Broken Open

Broken Open

Cynthia Carbone Ward

ISBN 978-0-578-43463-6

Printed in the United States of America

Published by Sacate Canyon Press

Front cover image by Kappy Wells.

Book cover design by Arlyn Nathan.

The author gratefully acknowledges the following permissions:

Canterbury Press, for permission to reprint an excerpt of the essay "Oremus" by Pádraig Ó Tuama, from his book *Daily Prayer with the Corrymeela Community*, 2017.

A.A. Knopf for permission to use an excerpt of the poem "Physics" by Sharon Olds, which appeared in a collection called *The Wellspring*, 1995.

Graywolf Press for permission to use an excerpt from "You Reading This, Be Ready" by William Stafford, from *Ask Me: 100 Essential Poems*. Copyright © 1980, 1998 by William Stafford and the Estate of William Stafford. Reprinted with the permission of The Permissions Company, Inc. on behalf of Graywolf Press, Minneapolis, Minnesota, www.graywolfpress.org.

For my steadfast companion

MONTE

"So let us pick up the stones over which we stumble,
friends, and build altars. Let us listen to the sound of breath
in our bodies. Let us listen to the sounds of our own voices,
of our own names, of our own fears. Let us name the harsh
light and soft darkness that surround us. Let's claw
ourselves out from the graves we've dug. Let's lick the earth
from our fingers. Let us look up and out and around. The
world is big and wide and wild and wonderful and wicked,
and our lives are murky, magnificent, malleable, and full of
meaning. Oremus. Let us pray."

– Pádraig Ó Tuama

Contents

PREFACE   xiii

PART I. BECOMING CONSCIOUS

1.   DETAILS   3

2.   TIES   7

3.   KNEE CAPS   11

4.   GOD   13

5.   WORK   19

6.   NO MAP   23

7.   THIEVERY   25

8.   A HOLIDAY PHOTO   29

9.   SOLSTICE   33

10. A SMALL PORTION OF EVENTS   37

11. PROSPECTS   41

12. TUESDAY AFTERNOON   45

PART II. A BLUR

13. TEACHING   *51*

14. MANATEE   *57*

15. ENGLAND   *61*

16. TIME IS A COUNTRY   *63*

17. A BRIGHTNESS   *67*

18. RECORDS   *69*

19. HEIRESS   *73*

20. A FRONT   *77*

21. ALMOST   *79*

PART III. I FIND MYSELF HERE

22. SIX TREES   *85*

23. HIDDEN CAVE   *93*

24. THIS PARTICULAR CREEK   *97*

25. JACKSON AND THE GOSPEL CHOIR   *101*

26. A SHIP PILED HIGH WITH ORANGES   *105*

27. TEXT MESSAGE   *111*

28. GIRL WITH A SUITCASE   *113*

29. THE WEIGHT OF THINGS   *117*

30. SHOOTING STARS   *123*

PART IV. BEARING WITNESS

31. HARBOR OF GRACE   *129*

32. ALIGNMENT 137

33. DAY TRIP 143

34. ROAD TRIP 147

35. BROKEN OPEN 161

36. THE WAY IT WAS 175

ACKNOWLEDGEMENTS & PERMISSIONS 179

About The Author 181

PREFACE

My grandfather Raffaele had a bungalow someplace, but all I can remember of it is a triangle of sunlight and faded sea green walls and the curlicue cadence of the words that it held. He and my father spoke Italian. They talked in the tempo of the south, a fervent and volatile kind of speech whose words never ended flat but spun in capricious dances through the air and concluded on magnificent mellifluous vowels. It was a sumptuous, sun-drenched language, and in its passionate rhythms I intuitively understood the punchy ardors of life. I wished my tongue would know this dance, wondered what the secrets were that could only be expressed in such a way.

But after my grandfather's death, he appeared to me in dreams; he spoke to me wordlessly, and I somehow understood. He told me about work, which is good in itself. He told me about love – fierce, irrational, and everlasting. He gave me his trust and his yearning, which I carry still. And he told me about outrageous hope that can stare down anything and never blink, hope that is born and reborn in a thousand incarnations. And I knew the secret language then, and I hugged him through his overcoat and time.

The themes that run through the essays in this collection are the very ones my grandfather handed down to me in that dialect of dreams. Although written across a range of twenty-five years and arising from different points and places in my journey –from child-hood days in New York to my current life on a California cattle ranch – I was surprised at the continuity they reveal. There is a before and after aspect to them simply because of the changes that accrue with time, and in particular because of an operation I underwent in February of 2018 that involved my brain and altered me profoundly. And yet, I have discovered that the shine of elemental truths is far more telling than the shifts. The pieces herein are linked by a sense of hope and love, reflecting my fluency in that language so long ago inscribed upon my heart.

I admit that I sometimes forgot what mattered, and maybe I needed a refresher course, and surely there was an easier way than having my head cut open and falling into an abyss, but I *really* get it now. I believe I have earned some authority to declare that things can get better, if we rise to the occasion. As the beloved poet William Stafford wrote, it is important that awake people be awake, "lest the parade of our mutual life get lost in the dark" – and it can be dark out there indeed. Today I am wide awake and paying attention, and I know it is essential that we connect to one another, encourage and reach out, notice and honor what is beautiful and good, and share our stories. These essays are my way of saying that the secret language is still res-onant, and that fundamental truths do not expire.

Let us never let go of the stance of love, integrity, and honesty – in our personal lives, and in the political, cultural, and societal realms as well. This terrible and wonderful world demands that we take the high road. Kindness and gratitude are the best impulses, and hope, as outrageous as it sometimes seems to be. Those same old stones across the stream are still strong and sturdy for stepping.

PART I

BECOMING

CONSCIOUS

"I woke up in bits, like all children, piecemeal over the years. I discovered myself and the world, and forgot them, and discovered them again…"

– Annie Dillard, *An American Childhood*

1

1

DETAILS

I didn't always know what street I was on, but I noticed stones and glitter embedded in the concrete, and sidewalk cracks to be avoided, and the chalky numbers of hopscotch games. I remember the glow of neon lights reflected in puddles, and window sills with clay pots of geraniums, and the stripes of sun and shade on the cool damp sand beneath the Coney Island boardwalk, where fleshy swimsuited bodies intertwined on blankets, and it smelled of salt and sweat and suntan oil and something cloyingly sweet, like cotton candy or corn dogs. I remember church bells clanging and traffic lights changing, the swish of brooms, the sing-song shouts of vendors peddling fish or offering to sharpen knives.

I remember people too, and vividly, like pictures in a gallery: a lady named Charlotte with watery eyes and parched pink skin who grew roses and gave them away, wrapping their thorny stems in damp paper towel. A brassy blonde named Blanche, with bracelets, bright lipstick, and manicured nails, an old friend of my mother's from before she was my mother, a discouraged person – somehow I could tell – but with a chipper veneer. There was easygoing Mr.

Keating, who might come downstairs and treat us all to ice cream when the Good Humor truck went by, and Rae Paterno, who served my mother coffee in the doughnut shop, lingering to chat if it wasn't busy, and Mr. Herman in the house of clocks, as stately and precise as a grandfather. There was nosy Mrs. Milici with her elbows on the window sill, and Charlie the butcher weighing liverwurst and packaging it in white paper, and Carol's Aunt Marie, being pulled along by her skinny, uncontrollable dog. There were so many people passing through whose names I didn't know, so many people living their lives, being busy, feeling what they felt. I remember the oddest details about them. It's just how my mind works. There's no cohesive whole, only details.

I recall details for navigating too, fragments of knowledge and advice, words left hanging in the air, maybe still there if I could go back to the place, close my eyes, and listen. Carol told me that a minute was longer than a moment. The crossing guard at Ocean Parkway said I should aspire to greater things. My brother told me never to let anyone see you cry, and he was partially right. I learned that tears could garner sympathy from people who loved me, but they gave power and satisfaction to the mean ones and were therefore best withheld.

I learned too that there was potent magic in pretending. The street could become anyplace you wanted it to be, games could engage you so fully they might as well be real. Carol and I pushed our baby dolls in prams along the leafy side streets with the stately porched houses – private, one-family homes – and it was as though we were all grown up and living there. My sisters and I were princesses in Prospect Park. No one could have told us otherwise. There was always a gap between fantasy and reality, but I had a knack for filling such gaps with stories. "You're such a Pollyanna," said my brother.

Christmastime came, and back then I perceived it in a silver-bells and snowflake kind of way, everything sparkling and hopeful, tinseled and twinkling, really quite conventional, "city sidewalks, busy sidewalks, dressed in holiday style", that sort of thing. But the season genuinely cheered me, and we were off from school. Salvation Army Santas rang their bells at storefronts, and we sang carols in church, which was a place I used to go. Women wore holiday corsages pinned to their coats: a cluster of ribbon and a sprig of pine, with perhaps a fake poinsettia and a plastic candy cane, and lots of glitter of course. I loved how strings of colored lights transformed even the shabbiest of houses, and there was a feeling that maybe this time my own troubled family would be like one in a storybook, with a tree and presents and everyone together, and no one would feel burdened or worried, and it wouldn't end in a terrible uproar.

I remember in great detail a particular day in December, walking with my mother. She was Jewish and had a different sense of this season-to-be-jolly, but it was pleasant being in the cold crisp air, everything festive and expectant. She wore her broad-shouldered wool coat and a felt beret she called a tam, which is how she used to dress then. That was my mother being young and beautiful, although I didn't realize it at the time.

We stopped to peer into a store window where Christmas corsages were on display, and just as I was wondering which one I would choose if ever I had the means for such a luxury, the proprietor of the shop stepped out onto the street with two corsages in his hand. I cannot recall his face, only his kindly demeanor. He was an older man, balding perhaps, bespectacled. He handed me a corsage and said, "Little girls should have corsages for the holiday."

Then, turning to give one to my mother, he said, "And pretty ladies too." He wished us a good day and a Merry Christmas, gave a courtly sort of bow, and retreated back into the shop. I spent the rest of the day feeling giddy, staring down at my corsage, touching its ribbons and tiny plastic charms, believing that I was now truly part of the pageantry and procession of Christmas in the city, right down to this detail on the lapel of my winter coat. I have no idea where in all of Brooklyn that store was or the name of that man, but I will never forget his gesture. He achieved a kind of immortality that day, and whoever he was, he is famous to me. He was one of those who helped me see the world as a place that could be gentle and unexpectedly indulgent.

It's easy to feel depressed and overwhelmed about the way things are, but maybe the idea is to think a little smaller sometimes. There were so many people hurrying by, living their lives, being busy, and some of them stopped to be kind. Those are the details that shape the world. What did it all mean? Are the answers in the details?

Details. I remember the details. And maybe I invent a few. But I can't recall the big picture at all, just a mosaic of details with many tiles missing.

2

TIES

When I was about four or five years old, my father went away on a trip to Florida. I only vaguely understood the purpose of the trip, but it was related to the construction or remodeling of a motel in St. Petersburg called The Marlin. My grandfather and my uncle, who were already there, had invested in this motel, and Daddy would be driving down with his friend and helper, Vito, and I understood that this was a work trip, not a vacation, but I felt a great surge of anticipatory abandonment nonetheless. I pictured palm trees and beaches and tropical skies, and my father in an exotic elsewhere far away, entirely minus me, being whoever he was without us.

The home of my childhood was a tumultuous one, and Daddy was our strength and our happiness, the heart of the universe as we knew it. I wanted to go with him. "I'll be back soon," he said. But soon seemed like a series of empty o's and moons and gloom. I went to the window that looked down on Coney Island Avenue, wept dramatically, then pulled myself together and decided to be a helper instead. I opened his suitcase, whose contents were austere, and looked in his closet in search of better choices. The best thing he had were his ties.

Oh, his beautiful ties! I couldn't even decide. I pulled down a sumptuous armful… gorgeous silky swaths of color: deep maroon, sapphire blue, a richly textured burgundy. They were striped or patterned in wondrous ways, classy but not bashful. Now these were adornments worthy of my father, who so often wore the paint-splattered overalls of the hardworking man he was, but who was also elegant and handsome, someone who enjoyed stepping out now and then feeling dressed-up and dapper.

And because I couldn't decide among the ties, I crammed them all into his suitcase. Why not be extravagant? I imagined him selecting one each morning, and it would shimmer like a jewel in the Florida sunshine, and he would emerge with new confidence. Or maybe it was just my way of going with him.

I suppose I've always had a fondness for ties. Decades later, I admired my husband's ties: bright flags among dark suits, a promising little crowd of prospects to choose among each morning. I had favorites: the one I bought him in Rome, with multiple hues of magenta; the retro one with a print of open fans; a bright red one with white flowers, so contrary to expectations. He doesn't often wear ties anymore, so he gathered most and donated them. He's very efficient about getting rid of things, too efficient sometimes. It was only by pure luck I was able to rescue a few, and I'm not sure what I will do with them, but I keep them with my arts and crafts supplies.

But, back to the 1950s, and my father's trip to Florida, and the ties I so helpfully packed. He of course opened the suitcase before he left, and he was not so much delighted as baffled and bemused. "Cheez," he said. (It was an exclamation he used. Some contraction of Jesus and cheese? It meant surprise, but with a dash of bewilderment.) "Who put all these ties in my suitcase?"

The answer to that was immediately apparent. He hugged me. But it would be hot and muggy in Florida, and it wasn't that kind of trip. He didn't take any ties with him. And in the end, I was glad. Because I could open his closet the whole time he was gone and bury my face in his ties.

3

KNEE CAPS

I walked to school each day when I was a kid in Brooklyn, a route of about ten blocks. It involved crossing Ocean Parkway, an impressively wide boulevard with a median in between lined with leafy trees and benches. Ocean Parkway was aptly named, since getting from one side to another was a little bit like going across a great sea, but a stalwart crossing guard stood ready to escort us and ensure our safety. Her name was Jeannette, and she had a French accent, and I wish I had been curious enough to ask her about her life, but she had a way of making me think that *I* was the interesting one. She always asked me about my day, and looked at my work, and seemed pleased and proud when I'd done well. Seeing Jeannette at Ocean Parkway was a highlight of my day.

One afternoon I showed her a drawing I'd done in class, a crayon and pencil rendition of what I'd intended to be a circus fat lady wearing a short red dance skirt.

"A fat lady?" said Jeannette. "Zees is no fat lady. Not skinny, no, but she is strong, not fat. Maybe she is the circus tightrope walker lady, eh?"

I was disappointed that my drawing hadn't conveyed what I'd envisioned, but Jeannette thought it was a very worthy effort. She pointed to the circus lady's knees, which I had represented with circular black swirls.

"Ah," she said, "you even gave her knee caps... such a fine detail. It shows you have an eye. You notice things. You are a very smart girl."

Jeannette stood tall in her wool navy coat and white gloves, a white reflective band across her chest. I admired her, and her opinion mattered... so much so that six decades later, here I am recalling her comments about my pencil rendering of knee caps and what it implied about my talent and intelligence.

I guess it's because Jeannette did so much more than get me safely across Ocean Parkway. She encouraged me and made me feel valued. She took her job seriously and added a whole new dimension to it. And when she asked me one day what I'd like to be when I grew up, I didn't hesitate: "A crossing guard."

"Oh, my goodness, no," she said, appalled. "You have to dream much, much better than zees."

In time I understood what she meant.

I am writing this to honor and thank not just Jeannette but all who bring heart and dignity to what might seem a trivial sort of job, and as a reminder that even small, routine encounters can touch someone deeply, and in a distant time and place they are remembered.

Jeannette gave me a little nudge and a little kindness, that's all... and helped me across the first of many seas. I eventually learned to dream better.

4

GOD

When I was a child, I heard an angel sing. Its voice was the most beautiful I had ever heard; it was silvery, like a river washing over me for a fleeting moment. Although I heard but a fragment, I understood that the song it sang was about a rose. I did not question this. I simply knew that I was not alone in my room.

I lived in a world in which spirits walked freely and doubt did not exist. There were angels on Coney Island Avenue and ghosts in Prospect Park. Borders blurred between dreams and waking, past and present. When I closed my eyes, I saw the starry flecks of a galaxy behind my eyelids. I heard the universe hum in the din of traffic and the rush of wind through treetops. There were oily rainbows in the gutters. God was wildly imaginative, even at times weird, but He took a personal interest in me.

Every night I prayed. My standard prayer was a lengthy, earnest litany which sometimes put me to sleep, but I never doubted that God heard, never doubted that He indulgently forgave me for the rudeness of dropping off in mid-sentence. My prayer was mostly about taking care of people, for there were many about whom I worried: my father worked too hard, my sister had kidney disease, my brother Eddie was always sad. I also blessed a lot of dead people, everyone from Grandma Assunta to Abraham Lincoln, and I was sure I would meet them all in heaven someday. I couldn't wait to ask Amelia Earhart where she'd been.

God got me to school before the bell, and like most kids at P.S. 179, I also prayed during class: "Please, God, don't let her call on me." He helped me through important tests, got me past the streets where nasty boys threw hard-packed snowballs, brought my paralyzed legs back to life one terrible morning when a man pulled me into an alley and shoved me against a wall and I froze in fear until God's hand gave a protective push and I ran free and fast into the morose security of the schoolyard.

I was a lapsed Catholic but did not know it. One day a woman named Ruby came to our house to draw us back into the flock at Holy Innocents. She was appalled that my belief system had grown so expansive and liberal. She told me that I must kneel beside my bed when I pray, that God did not hear such lazy, sleepy prayers as mine. She said that God expected to see me in mass on Sunday. My negligent parents were hell-bound already, but for me there was hope if I followed the rules.

My mother, a Jew who married an Italian, was disdainful. "Those Catholics are too strict," was her assessment, she who had been disowned by her family for marrying a Gentile. But her tribe had a long history of exile. I saw it in the sad eyes of the old women who huddled together in the park speaking Yiddish; I saw it in the tattooed numbers on the arm of the tailor and his wife.

My mother's form of Judaism was a lonely and mystical one. She lit candles in glasses and taught me to kiss the mezuzah that was mounted on our wall like a magic charm, but these artifacts were lifeless oddities to me, like things in a museum. Her God had turned away in anger, leaving her to fend for herself, and I was the child of an ill-fated union that everyone had spoken against.

One day, my best friend Carol Bessey invited me to accompany her to St. Mark's Methodist Church. It was a congenial place, and I soon felt like an adopted daughter there, signing up for Sunday school, choir, and a religious instruction group that met every Wednesday afternoon. The God at this address was an affable one, a firm handshake kind of God, a constructive social activist, fond of potlucks, rummage sales, and summer camp for city kids. In His beautiful sanctuary, well-dressed citizens gathered together singing hymns that became dear and familiar to me. There were lilies on the altar. Rose-toned sunlight slanted through the stained-glass windows.

The agonized Christ that the Catholics were fixed upon was absent from St. Mark's. Instead, there was Jesus, who seemed loving and humble, a gentle teacher. At his head, there was always a yellow circle of light, but I felt the humanity of this Jesus, cried at his suffering, rejoiced at the happy outcome of Easter, and fervently hoped it was all true.

Jesus was the ultimate role model, and I knew I had to try to be good. Even a child, after all, makes himself known by his acts. This high-minded quest was to be forever accompanied by feelings of guilt and inadequacy, for I discovered I could be pretty grabby when it came to earthly goods, and occasionally I was inexplicably bad, like when I stole a pair of doll shoes from the Woolworths on Flatbush Avenue or turned off the light and locked Mary Ellen into the bath-room just to give her a scare. And although I deliberately did kind things, too, I had inherited a terrible temper and was not big on for-giveness prior to revenge. In the end, I only hoped the good in me would outweigh the bad.

I still felt the constant presence of my original God, still knew He did not dwell exclusively in one particular house. And though billions of other souls had claim on him, I never doubted that He looked out for me in some special way. I added the Lord's Prayer to my silent monologues and felt forgiven every night for all of my trespasses. I was distracted now, and growing up, but a ring of ritual encircled me. I had known a few storms, survived them, and felt safe.

But years passed. My own invulnerable father abruptly died one October night while I was far away. My sister's disease worsened, my brother lost his mind, and the furies of the world raged on. There was not a shred of evidence that anything existed beyond the bleak present to make sense of all the suffering. The dead grew more dead each day, and my God had wandered off into another universe, or maybe He was preoccupied, or maybe He had simply never been.

I came upon a quote by Émile Durkheim: "If God did not exist, it would be necessary to invent him." These words disturbed me more than anything I had ever read, for suddenly I suspected that indeed it had been necessary, and if God was not a human invention, I wanted a sign. But none was forthcoming. Not even Daddy could break through. If doubt was a sin, I prayed for forgiveness, for the only thing I believed with certainty was that nothing could be certain. Now I was the exile, banished from the infinite, relegated to the secular world of rocks and buildings. Everything had grown smaller.

I recalled my father's strong arms pushing me high in a swing in Prospect Park long ago at dusk. As I soared through the summer air, I had seen the tiny lanterns of a hundred fireflies, felt the joy of the wind, trusted so completely that I would return safely back to Daddy's hands that I didn't even think about it. I simply sailed with abandon, leaning back to see the sky, freed by my faith. And thus had I started out life. When did flying become falling?

And why did I suddenly require tangible proof of the unimaginable? How ungrateful I was for the many years God had been within me and without me, both intimate and limitless. I began to see that I might in some small way reflect God like a mirror. If I found it in my heart to forgive myself, then perhaps I might be forgiven. If I led a life of love, perhaps I was not inventing a loving God, but emulating one. If I chose to believe there was more than I could see, there was more than I could see. Perhaps it was not God who had turned away, but me.

"Learn slowly and ask questions," advised a Muslim friend named Kassim, "because all of the answers will point to the truth."

I ask. I look around, too, and my questions linger unresolved, but I've grown used to ambiguity, and what I lack in conviction I more than make up for in hope. But I'm quite convinced that if God exists, He isn't fond of churches based on intolerance or doctrine enforced by cruelty. 'That is not what I meant," I can picture Him saying, "That is not what I meant at all."

Then again, maybe it's better to stop asking, and just listen. My wise friend Dan quotes Angelus Silesius "God, whose love is present everywhere, can't come to visit unless you are not there."

Dan speculates that we are all angels (or Buddhas) in the undistracted moments when we are simply *being,* unencumbered by the notion of a substantial self, immersed in everyday meditations – like walking the dog or watching the clouds or writing a poem. For Dan, a poet, it's inseparable from poetry, "a self-forgetful, perfectly useless concentration," as Elizabeth Bishop described the conditions necessary for creating or appreciating art. "I wish you many such moments," Dan has written to me.

And sometimes I *do* absent myself, making room for a visit, and love becomes a palpable presence. Sometimes, too, I sense the pulsating heart of the organism that is earth, and my soul is like water, clear and uncontained, and I cannot find the words for this.

But when I was a child, I heard the silvery voice of an angel, and I am certain it was real.

5

WORK

My father aspired to be a doctor. I still have in my possession a letter from St. Francis College outlining the requirements for a pre-med course of study, sent in response to his hopeful inquiry. The 1920s were drawing to a close, the stock market was about to crash, and our nation would soon plunge into the Great Depression that was so formative in the lives of our parents' generation. But my father's family was already poor. His immigrant father struggled to make a living, his mother was ill and frail, and life did not allow for luxuries like college.

The eldest of four brothers, one of whom died at the age of four, my father was brilliant and motivated and knew the value of higher learning, but many dreams dissolved in the rooms of their railroad flat in a gritty neighborhood of Brooklyn. He managed to take a few classes, read voraciously on his own, and wrote and spoke with unusual eloquence, but he finally picked up the buckets and brushes of his father's humble trade. He still yearned for a respected profession, and he certainly had the heart and ability to be a wonderful physician, but he took the jobs that came his way, added murals and decorative effects to the drudgery of basic wall painting, and never had a break. He labored until the day he died at the age of sixty-seven.

I remember him coming home at night in paint-splattered overalls and paint-splattered shoes, washing and grooming and emerging as the handsome and dignified gentleman he was. In those early years when we still lived in the city, he would leave the house to attend night classes at the Atlantic States Chiropractic Institute, and even though I was only a little girl, I sensed his noble determination and felt proud of him. He completed the program with distinction and was forever after *Dr.* Carbone, a legitimate, hard-earned title, even if he painted houses by day.

It was difficult to start a viable practice as a chiropractor in an era when the profession was often dismissed as quackery, and especially for a man who was working long hours to support a family weighed down by more than its fair share of adversity. He grew tired. Now he came home exhausted, lay down in bed, and often fell asleep with his eyeglasses on and an open book that had slipped from his hands to his chest. I tiptoed in once and gently removed his glasses, and my heart swelled with a huge, protective, overwhelming love.

But I was useless. Being young is an all-consuming career, and I had not inherited his vision or his drive. He warned me that the clock was ticking and that I needed to advance myself, get a degree, become someone in the world. Become a doctor, in fact... by which he meant M.D., for he still saw that as the pinnacle profession, and he knew that I could do it. Unfortunately, I had zero interest in becoming a doctor, nor did I seek to define and pursue whatever it was that interested me. I thought I had plenty of time to figure things out.

And in the meantime, I can see how he shielded me, doing things for all of us that we should have been learning to do for ourselves.

Somehow he would manage to find an old car for me, and somehow he arranged to keep it maintained, and somehow there would be cash in an envelope to pay for my gas. It shames me now to think of it. He was trained in the crucible of hard work and taking care of others. It was all he knew. And he was a force of nature, a one-man industry for betterment, constantly repairing things, solving problems, even cooking and cleaning the house.

In fact, it's his housecleaning proclivity that my childhood friend, Carol, remembered about him. I had a phone conversation with her recently, the first time I had heard her voice in fifty years, and she mentioned a memory of my father from our Coney Island Avenue days. "I have an image of him sweeping and mopping the stairs and the lobby," she said. "I remember it in such detail. He used one of those mops made of string, but what I especially remember is the pail. It was one of those tin pails with a wringer inside, a very nice pail, and he worked with care, like it mattered. Your father really tried to take care of things."

He sure did. And when Carol described it, I could almost smell the pine-scent of disinfectant, an odd aroma to associate with love, but I do. I could see the tile floor of the little vestibule where Carol and I sometimes sat and played with our dolls until the landlady hollered at us to get out of people's way, not that there were any people. And I could see the steep wooden stairs that led to our apartment on the first floor, and the narrow dim hallway. My father kept it clean for us.

Oh, there were probably a hundred more impressive things for which my father might have preferred to be remembered, even by his daughter's childhood friend. She might have seen how imposing and handsome he looked when he stepped out in his suit, how smart and well-spoken he was, how generous. And there was the respectful way people asked him for advice and referred to him as *Doc*, and the fact that he passed even his X-ray licensing exam, and that he moved listeners to tears when he drove up to Albany and addressed the Assembly of the State of New York about an issue that mattered to him deeply. Carol didn't know, either, how he painted the walls of our rooms with flowers and birds, making everything more beautiful, and cooked us tomato sauce and lentil soup, and washed our hair and tucked us in, and shelved his own dreams to give us all the chances he hadn't had, and fortified us with courage.

My daughter once copied these lines from a poem called *Physics* by Sharon Olds, and gave them to me, and it occurred to me that this is how I view my father too:

> *Now she tells me*
> *that if I were sitting in a twenty-foot barn,*
> *with the doors open at either end,*
> *and a fifty-foot ladder hurtled through the barn*
> *at the speed of light, there would be a moment*
> *—after the last rung was inside the barn*
> *and before the first rung came out the other end—*
> *when the whole fifty-foot ladder would be*
> *inside the twenty-foot barn, and I believe her,*
> *I have thought her life was inside my life*
> *like that.*

I don't know how he fits, but yes, he is inside my life like that forever. My father, whose savings totaled eleven dollars when he died, taught me everything I need to know of greatness and dignity, and he filled me with love that I draw upon still. He wanted most of all to be a physician, but in the end, he was so much more than that, and the poignant image of him humbly mopping the stairs takes on new meaning to me. I am proud to be the daughter of this worker.

6

NO MAP

He was my brother, and the country of childhood was a tangled one, fraught with discord and shadowed by mystery. Dangers loomed, whether real or imagined, and tranquil moments could not entirely be trusted, for they were as delicate as glass and might easily shatter. But he knew how to make me laugh, and he taught me many things: the refuge of crayon and pencil retreats, the magic of pretending to be someone else, and how marks on a page can transform into words and everything suddenly shines.

There was no map for that country, but we walked it together. He knew the names of all the dinosaurs, and he took arty pictures with his little Brownie camera, and he salvaged a red bicycle that someone had thrown away and showed me the momentum and mobility in that humble machine. He told me once that we should never let anyone see us cry. I had discovered somewhere along the way that my tears could garner sympathy and attention, so I indulged in them with vigor when I felt like, but my brother endured all with stoic dignity. His suffering was real, and life was brutally unfair, but I never saw him cry, and I never saw him mean.

In time he went elsewhere, living among strangers or in lonely rooms, trying hard to attain outcomes that for so many others had simply been written into the script. He completed a degree in economics and even started law school far away. He was brilliant and creative, but he was born with a terrible kidney disease and it finally took its toll... life on dialysis, poverty, confusion. He wandered, he was hospitalized more than once, he called me from bus stations in implausible places, and went back at the end to our family home. It wasn't much of a home by then, and there wasn't much of a welcome, but where was he to go?

He was my protector, and over time I had grown taller and stronger than him, and I should have become *his* protector, but of course I failed to do so. His letters kept coming, to me and to my daughter, who was only a baby, but he hoped someday she would read them and know her Uncle Eddie. He never felt well, not ever, but he sent her paper fans and plastic figurines, children's books and collectible coins, boxes of cookies and his own ink drawings. My brother had so little, but his heart was so generous.

And it was his heart that finally failed him, a secondary development in kidney disease. Corrective surgery was attempted, in a New York City hospital, and he never recovered. I have a letter he wrote me a day or two before the surgery, looking out the window at the city lights, still filled, despite everything, with hopes and promises, or maybe he was just trying to be brave. I will never know. He was forty-five when he died.

I am writing this on his birthday. He would have been seventy years old. I have never learned what to do with my sadness. There is no map for this country.

7

THIEVERY

One day more than sixty years ago I went with my grandfather to the Brooklyn Botanical Gardens, just the two of us, which happened no more than once or twice in all of time. I was a four-year-old brat, unhappy for all sorts of reasons I would have been too young to articulate, and my grandfather was preoccupied and quiet. Even at that age, I could sense that he was not particularly fond of me, which in retrospect I can understand, but I didn't know how to win him over. There was something inaccessible about him, and it would be many years and much too late before I thought about all the questions I wish I had asked him.

I wore a heavy, coarse wool jacket, bomber style, zippered, plaid. The early spring sun felt warm on my face, and there was bird song, the fragrance of blossoms, a lazy feeling. We had wandered through a greenhouse together, humid and tropical inside, and I would forever after love such places and associate them with my grandfather. But now we had exited the greenhouse and nothing was happening; I was bored and antsy and craving a what-next. My amorphous discontent turned to delight when I noticed a comic book lying on a bench.

It was a *Felix the Cat* comic, a special edition, small and thick, the size of a paperback book. I ran over and picked it up, flipped a few pages, and immediately assumed ownership. It would be fun to carry around and peruse at my leisure, a found treasure that even my older brothers would envy.

A young boy approached the area as we were walking away, and somehow I knew that his mission was to retrieve the comic book. He looked beyond us purposefully, certain that he had left it on the bench, not noticing that it was in my hand. My grandfather whispered to me in his bumpy broken English that the comic book belonged to the boy and I needed to return it.

I wish I could tell you otherwise, but I was obnoxious and indignant. Finders keepers, that sort of thing. The book had been abandoned and it was meant to be mine. My grandfather looked at me with a kind of weary resignation, his babysitting duties thankfully almost over, and rather than have to deal with my whining, he deftly took the book from my hand and slipped it under my jacket.

Had he learned this trick stealing bread as a boy from some Neapolitan street vendor, lifting sausage from a butcher shop, absconding with fruit from an orchard not his? He had executed the motion with such cool and expertise. Now I felt the book snug against my chest, and I moved stiffly to keep it in place.

The boy looked at me accusingly. I saw him say something to his mother and point at me. But my grandfather's presence gave me an aura of innocence and respectability I didn't deserve. An old man would surely not facilitate a petty theft or condone such dishonest behavior. Neither the boy nor his mother confronted us. I had made my grandfather an accomplice to my crime, and we had gotten away with it.

In the end, of course, I didn't enjoy possessing the *Felix the Cat* book, and I couldn't understand why I had wanted it so much. Even as we walked through the gates of the botanical garden, I had an impulse to let it slip from my jacket and fall to the ground, and I would have gladly left it there to be trampled by feet and rained upon. But on some level I understood that my grandfather had compromised his ethics to appease my want and shut me up, and I didn't want him to see how little the coveted comic meant to me now. I owned it, and I owned the sordid history of its acquisition, and these were heavy things to carry. My grandfather wasn't proud of me *or* himself that day, and somewhere in Brooklyn there was a boy who had seen me for the unscrupulous little crook that I was.

It was a lesson in honesty and integrity taught in reverse. I learned that the value and pleasure in a thing is inextricably linked to how it was obtained. I learned that shame has weight. I learned that the stone facade of my grandfather could be worn down by petulance, but this would never yield his love or the secrets of his past.

8

A HOLIDAY PHOTO

The photograph was taken in December of 1962, and my only clue that it was the Christmas season is the decorated tree behind us, a scrawny thing, but it represents an effort. (I note that there are even a few wrapped presents at the base.) The seated older man in tie and sweater is my paternal grandfather Raffaele, with Rose, his second wife, at his side. Seated on the floor is my father, holding my youngest sister Libbie, then me in the middle with my beloved cat Colonel, and my other sister, Marlene. It's a picture that tells many stories, both in what is seen and in what – or who – is missing.

Among the missing are my brothers. Where were the boys? And my mother, unless it is she who took the picture, but there was never a reshuffling for a shot that would include her, and there is a lingering sense of exile attached to her. This is about as close as we ever got to a family gathering. There was always someone gone or something wrong, some disaster in progress or pending. But oh, how we tried! I think that's what makes it all so poignant. Everyone had such good intentions and lofty aspirations.

1962. We had moved from the city that summer, and this was

our first Christmas in our Long Island house. It was a good brick 1920s house on a lot still edged with woods. I remember the uneven stucco wall surface of the living room, and its main feature, the fireplace, which we would never use. The peculiar semi-circle couch had once resided in the waiting room of my father's by-then-defunct chiropractic office in Brooklyn. It was orange, a unique mid-century piece, its pedestal perfect for piling magazines, or in this case placement of a small Christmas tree.

My grandfather's visit would have made this an occasion. I can see that my father, always in charge and overworked, is trying to orchestrate things, his hands in the midst of some instructional gesture, probably telling Libbie to look up at the camera, the fatigue in his eyes barely concealed. Of course, my dear sister Marlene chose to wear her patent leather shoes and to hold her palms together as though in prayer. There's nothing accidental in that – she had a sense of ceremony and undoubtedly felt that a religious pose would be appropriate for a picture commemorating this holy time of year. (She was full of songs, too, and gifted with a beautiful voice.)

Meanwhile Rose, who was never loved by any of my grandfather's sons (yet another story) is looking towards my grandfather, the only one who would have wanted her there, and he is speaking to her exclusively, his gaze downward, both a part of the group and apart. As for me, I still possessed the sweet and earnest face of an eleven-year-old idealist. I was eager and kind and held my heart forward for all the world to see, just as I held my cat.

I came across this photo, among other odd finds, in the midst of "curating" my computer files, a seemingly interminable task. I was taking a break from the material accumulations I have yet to tackle: shoeboxes filled with old photos and negatives, stacks of letters and memorabilia in the downstairs closet, the "trunk of pain" in the garage. I thought that sorting through my digital mess would be a more manageable undertaking that might nonetheless yield a nice sense of accomplishment, and by and large, that's been the case. But then there are scanned images like this one that pull me in and take me away to places I had no intention of revisiting, and suddenly I am Alice in the rabbit hole, falling fifty-six years deep.

Bursting up from the tunnel I behold the present, a tricky year in its almost-over stage, one day after Winter Solstice, with a drizzly kind of rain – light and straight-down – no wind. It is so oddly still that at times the droplets seem to hover in the air like mist, but now and then there's a lemon slice of sudden sunlight, and the road shines like a silver ribbon. 'Tis the season, and as always, it's a mixed bag, crammed as full of yearning as it is with festivity, and terribly hard for some.

But when I choose to move beyond the loss and sadness, which though very conspicuous is *not* the only outcome, I find an unexpected message within this old Christmas photo. If my father was sustained by dreams that failed to materialize, the days warmed by those dreams are not retracted, the disappointment does not diminish the comfort they brought while their promise and truth seemed viable. If my sister sang songs and held her palms in prayer, that happened, and nothing can extinguish the wonder of it. If my heart was kind and hopeful then, who is to say it changed?

I picture us casting away the burdens of sorrow and regret until nothing remains but gratitude and forgiveness, which are pure and clear and utterly weightless, and our souls are so light we can fly. The saga is unbound by linear terms, and it's happening still, and it breathes within me, as real as my own pulse. For lack of a better term, I shall title it love. And it endures.

9

SOLSTICE

Central Islip was a working-class Long Island town of cheap lumber houses and small vistas. It seems we were always in search of a place to hide, to render ourselves separate from its oppressive dullness. Once Rosemary and I found a hidden creek beneath an overpass of Veteran's Highway. We clambered down with candy bars in our hands and sat there for hours, pretending to be someplace else. When we were lucky, we would manage a ride to a nearby beach, loving the fact that there was indeed an end to the grim crisscross of empty streets, a physical edge to look beyond. A friend drove us one day to a road with the enchanting name of Crystal Brook Hollow. It led us to the Long Island Sound, and there we listened to the lull of water lapping onto pebbled shore.

And at Robert Moses State Park on Fire Island, anyone who was willing to walk a hundred yards could still find solitude. People clustered near the parking lots and restrooms, renting umbrellas, placing coolers and blankets on the white sand, building noisy communities that somehow replicated the clamor of daily life. But I was willing to walk. I knew there was an old lighthouse further west at Point

Democrat, as well as the remains of a shambling dwelling built of planks and driftwood – a place where one could live for a summer. I fantasized about that. I would be a cross between Huck Finn and Pippi Longstocking, clever and autonomous. I would write songs and wear my hair in braids. I would watch the storms gather over the sea, endure their pounding rains, and never be afraid.

Lilacs were more fragrant then. All rain was hard, every star shimmered, the wind through the treetops was a voice in my ear, and each path through the sparse scrub woods might yet lead to someplace undiscovered. I yearned to see the sun rise over the sea, and one Summer Solstice morning, my boyfriend Richie – who was nineteen years old and drove a VW Beetle – agreed to take me to Robert Moses Park at dawn. I knew my father would never understand. I agreed to sneak out of the house in the dark of 4 a.m. and meet Richie a little further down the street. We drove across the Causeway just as the first sun of summer began to rise like a great flat coin above the water.

And that was it. We watched the sunrise, vowed never to forget this particular June morning, and Richie dropped me off at my house. The sky had lost its blush by now, but still possessed its early morning shyness. I stood for a long while in the backyard, fully awake and unwilling to return to my bed. A single rose had emerged from a small thorny bush I had inexpertly planted myself. I examined it like a proud mother, then sat on our brick steps and stroked the fur of an old cat named Duke who belonged to nobody but frequented our yard. I enjoyed the way Duke unquestioningly accepted my unlikely presence in the morning's narrow seam, pushing his thick head against me, purring at my unexpected companionship.

Suddenly the door opened, and my father appeared. He wore a green plaid flannel shirt and old paint-splattered trousers, and he car-

34

ried a thermos of coffee. A single shank of his black hair fell across his forehead, and he looked at me with a bemused, tired expression. For an instant I braced myself for defense, but he knew nothing of my foray to the beach, and I could tell he was happy to see me. He smiled as though my being there was nothing more than a pleasant surprise that did not require explanation. I realized only then how bleak and lonely were his mornings. No one rose to make him breakfast or see him off, even in the dark of winter. Sometimes I would wake and hear him getting ready downstairs. There would be a small clatter of keys and kitchen things, then the door would shut, and he would drive away, and I would lie there as the sky grew light and blank, feeling utterly bereft until my trifling dreams reclaimed me.

Now he smiled and reached for me, and I nestled my head into his shirt the way I had when I was a little girl. He smelled vaguely of coffee and casein paint, and his shirt was soft and achingly familiar, and he had about him a residue of sleep and weariness that made him gentle. I felt protective of him suddenly, and it occurred to me on some guttural level that he would not be with me forever, and my heart chilled with a fleeting foreknowledge that I was not capable of grasping.

"It's the first day of summer, Daddy."

"No kidding," he said distractedly, as though all days were one smudged procession.

"I couldn't sleep," I added, "so I thought I'd get up and greet the day."

I wondered if my father ever felt the restlessness that stirred in me, the romantic tug of wanderlust and yearning. It would be many years and much too late before I found the letters and poems he had penned in his youth. *If I could but scale tonight the vault of sky,* one poem began, *the stars as stepping stones to reach on high...*

But I suppose I thought I'd invented yearning. I somehow assumed that my father had been programmed differently to choose this life.

"Well, kid," he said, beginning to shift, "you got to greet an old man, too." He pronounced it *keed,* as he always did when he called me this. It was an affectionate nickname, and it pleased me.

He approached the car and turned to me once more. "Help out today, and take care of the baby," he said, referring to my two-year old brother, who was already beginning to dislike the label.

"Daddy…" I don't know what it was that pressed upon my heart. I did not yet know the names for love and had never felt this weight, this vast presence at the core of me, so elemental I might dissolve within it or die without it. I was frightened and grateful, immobilized by the enormity of what seemed both burden and gift. In time, I would get used to this, for my heart would fold over it, and my soul would take its shape, but for now, I was suspended precariously in the stilled breath of morning. It was the start of summer, and I was sixteen.

10

A SMALL PORTION OF EVENTS

Robert was my friend, though I never realized what a gift that was. We were in many of the same classes and took the same bus to school and circumstances tossed us together often enough that we developed a comfortable way of being close that didn't imply anything more. He was, to use a phrase that somehow diminishes its value, a 'nice guy' – gracious and kind even in his teens. Once, for example, when Louise's boyfriend decided to have a birthday party for her, Robert joined forces with him on my behalf after learning that my birthday was just a day before Louise's, thus turning it into a party for me too. Why? Because he didn't want me to feel left out, and he thought it would be fun, and anyway, weren't we all good friends?

Long Island in those days was still a sleepy place with woods around the edges, and we ourselves were not yet fully born. We imagined that wider horizons would open up to us someday and great possibilities awaited, but Robert didn't intend to be passive about it. He wanted to go places and *do* things. He was interested, enthusiastic, and full of ideas.

In 1964, the World's Fair arrived in Flushing, Queens, and at

Robert's suggestion we uncharacteristically abandoned school in order to take the train into the city and check it out. It was a phantasmagoria: we watched atoms collide at the General Electric exhibit, journeyed into space in the Hall of Science, flew to the moon in an easy chair courtesy of General Motors, saw ourselves on color television at RCA, and then zipped above it all in a futuristic monorail. At the Coca Cola exhibit we walked together through a humid Cambodian rainforest, a noisy street in Hong Kong, an Alpine ski lodge that smelled of snow and peppermint. We watched a puppet show in Paris, glimpsed the Tivoli Gardens in miniature, stepped on an escalator that moved us slowly past Michelangelo's *Pietà*, its white marble lit eerily against a blue backdrop. There was an automated Abe Lincoln, a Sinclair dinosaur, and a friendly carburetor named Carby, a name Robert took to calling me.

Perhaps tellingly, one of my favorite exhibits at the fair was the Parker Pen Pavilion, where we filled out questionnaires that would lead us to a perfect pen pal. (I lied in the hopes of being matched with a cute English guy – the 'British Invasion' was in full swing after all – but instead I got a wonderful girl from the Netherlands named Tiny Bisschops; we wrote to each other for many years before somehow losing contact, and I wish I could find her again.) The theme of the fair was 'Peace Through Understanding' and despite the vaguely worrisome display of global population growth at Equitable Life Assurance, it presented a breathtakingly optimistic view of the world, American industry at the helm. This was fine with Robert and me, for we were setting sail into that world, and it was nice to anticipate blue skies and the wind at our backs, a few challenges, of course, but nothing that technology, innovation, and spirit couldn't handle. 'America is never accomplished,' declared the inscription at the Federal Pavilion. We would be busy and purposeful.

One day another Robert came to town: Bobby Kennedy was running for the Senate and bringing his campaign to Long Island. He had a scheduled stop in Central Islip, and it was Robert who knew this was an occasion not to be missed, for he had a sense of history that I lacked, a sense of event. And so we walked downtown and stood among the crowds that lined the main street, and there, atop a vehicle or platform of some kind, was RFK himself, his hair a thick shock of sandy brown, his features youthful and handsome, smiling and waving and reaching down to accept the hands offered up to him, including my own. I shook hands with Bobby Kennedy. And I would follow his career and hear his words even as the shadows on our land became harder to ignore, and conflicts escalated, and dreams grew more complex.

"Few will have the greatness to bend history itself," he said, "but each of us can work to change a small portion of events, and in the total of all those acts will be written the history of this generation."

We were the class of '68, Robert and I, and we all know how things went for America that year: another wrong-headed war raged on, and in April Dr. King was murdered, and in June, two weeks before our high school graduation, Kennedy was shot in the kitchen of the Ambassador Hotel while seeking the Democratic nomination for president. I was seventeen and barely on the brink of understanding. Lost in my personal confusions, I drifted into a private world that felt challenging enough at the time.

After graduation, I never saw Robert again.

He called me once, twenty years later. He had somehow discovered that we were both on the West Coast, not quite neighbors, but relatively close: I was living in Laguna Beach and he in Los Angeles. He worked as a costume designer and wardrobe supervisor for a popular television show, and he was proud of that.

"Watch for my name on the credits," he said, and I did, many times, and it was true.

He did not seem to look back on our Long Island years with affection or nostalgia. "There were some small minds in our town," he said. "They're still there, probably."

Robert was a man who had gotten out, and was successful, and felt vindicated somehow. He wanted me to know that. As for me, I was just excited that he had called, and I felt a great surge of warmth and encouraged him to visit me, but even as we said good-bye I sensed this was unlikely.

More recently, I wondered yet again if there was a chance that Robert and I might reconnect somehow. Stories never end for me, and I don't like to lose track of people. I typed his name into Google, and a single article appeared. It had been published in *Variety* in 1992 – an obituary. Robert was forty-two years old when he died.

But Robert was my friend, and nothing can change that fact. We stood side by side at a remarkable moment in history, and we watched it all with hope and wonder. We each endured our private pain and enjoyed our separate achievements. With naïveté and awe, we imagined the future, succeeded, failed, continued, and influenced our own small portion of events. I have no doubt Robert dreamed of things that never were, and he surely asked why not.

PROSPECTS

It was 1971, late summer or early fall, and in my memory the day is cast in an amber kind of glow, all warm hues and soft edges. I was twenty years old, a college dropout, still snagged on some rickety splintered bridge between little girl and functional adult. I had recently returned to our family home on Long Island to figure out what to do next; my boyfriend in medical school waited in Chicago, his offer of marriage only vaguely answered. On this particular day I had accompanied my father to Brooklyn, where he had a couple of business appointments. He dropped me off on Flatbush Avenue to wander until he was done.

There was a sign advertising a big sale in the dress department of a bargain basement store and I went in to take a look. The clothes were cheaply made and basic, but I figured I could use a new dress if I decided to go back to Chicago, or even if not, and the seven-dollar price tag was convincing. I chose one in beige, a soft jersey fabric, and very short, which was the style. It seemed easy to wear and versatile, and its neutral generic-ness didn't hem it in to any particular purpose. I could wear it to work if I got a job, or out on the town if

I ever went anyplace, or to a marriage civil ceremony, if things went that way. I counted out the bills and carried it off, a soft heap of fabric in a small paper bag.

I walked along the street carrying my plain-wrap new dress, feeling inexplicably pleased with myself, and thinking I might stop for a cold soda, or meander over to Prospect Park. It was a beautiful day. Sunshine drenched the city, store windows gleamed, sidewalks glittered. People were moving slowly, as though they knew this moment would never come again. There was something dreamlike about it; my worries receded, and it didn't seem to matter so much what I'd be doing next. I felt I had prospects, even if just by virtue of being young and alive. I felt equipped.

I noticed a young man standing on a corner, reading a map, his knapsack propped against a lamppost. He looked up, said hello, and seemed willing to loiter and chat. Spencer was his name, and he was visiting from Sydney, Australia, a place so remote I could barely imagine it. He was older than me, though not by much, and handsome in a nothing-special way, handsome the way my new dress was wearable, with even features, an easy smile, nothing promised, but nothing excluded. Spencer had no particular agenda, and he wondered what I'd recommend he see while he was here. We walked a bit, with no destination in mind, and we talked about everything, in the way that confidences sometimes spill out with a stranger. We enjoyed each other's company.

Spencer seemed an emissary from a faraway continent, and I sensed some deeper significance in our unlikely meeting at this odd junction of my life. I found his accent refreshing and appreciated his nonchalant aura of adventure and travel. I pictured ferries and railroad tickets, luggage on docks, a well-worn passport in the pocket of faded dungarees. Heck, maybe I'd even visit him in Australia one day. Would I like to see Australia? I had an invitation now. And just because it had never occurred to me, that didn't mean it couldn't happen. There was a whole world out there, and Spencer radiated with possibilities.

Oh, I wish I could say that I ran away with Spencer, or even that we spent the day together. But my father would be back at two to pick me up, and despite the glimmers of defiance in me, my default position was compliance and resignation. And I'd like to tell you that I said no to marrying the boyfriend in Chicago, but it seemed like the line of least resistance at the time, an easy way out, although it wasn't. In less than a month, I would be wearing my beige mini-dress at the Cook County Courthouse, becoming the wife of the medical student. I would spend that night crying and the next few years leaving, and a decade of confusion would ensue. It was a necessary detour, I suppose.

But for a few minutes on Flatbush Avenue in 1971, music drifted from doorways, traffic thrummed, sunshine washed over me, and I was a golden creature who could have stepped right through the wide-open door of the world. I was very young and had not yet ruined anything irrevocably.

Instead I boarded the train of inevitabilities for which I'd been programmed, looking back only once as I left. Spencer stood there shining like a stack of untold stories.

12

TUESDAY AFTERNOON

It was the depths of the 1970s, and I was taking classes at the state university in Albany. One semester more and I'd have a degree, and that would mean I'd finally accomplished something, or so I'd been led to believe. I was renting a room above a dry cleaner's in a place that always smelled like solvent when it didn't smell like something unappealing being fried in the kitchen on a cast iron pan by one of the two young women with whom I shared the apartment, both of them lonely and peculiar, and I guess this was where I belonged.

I was still romancing an alcoholic professor in Syracuse, and I'd had a fight with him before boarding the bus back to Albany, and there was nothing unusual about this except that he'd swung a punch at me this time, and I'd made my exit with drama and pathos, filled with outrage and self-pity in equal parts and sporting a black eye. Actually, black is a misnomer – the bruising was closer to purple. But I had friends, and one of them, a medical student, had given me a couple of pills called Quaaludes. This will relax you, he said, and oh, did it ever.

So I was back in my room above the dry cleaner's in Albany relaxing with my Quaalude. I remember that a particular song was spinning on the record player: "Tuesday Afternoon" by the Moody Blues, either a very long version of it, or over and over in an endless loop. (If you survived the seventies, you know the song too.)

Pretentious and over-orchestrated is how one impromptu critic described the music of the Moody Blues, and someone else referred to adolescent lyrics trying too hard to sound profound, but I liked it, and in my Quaalude state of mind, "Tuesday Afternoon" playing over and over was a custom-made anthem and a personal lullaby, the song to which I'd restart my life or sleep it all away.

It happened to be Tuesday, even. How's that for serendipity?

Tuesday afternoon.
I'm just beginning to see,
Now I'm on my way.
It doesn't matter to me,
Chasing the clouds away.

Whatever it meant, those were my feelings exactly, especially the "it doesn't matter to me" part because really, nothing did. I was all druggy and drowsy, lying in my narrow bed with a view of the bookie joint grocery store across the street and the eerie glow of a neon sign flickering on as daylight slid into evening, with the smells of dry-cleaning fluid and frying onions wafting through the rooms... and someone knocking at the door.

It was Jack, a grad student, Vietnam vet, casual friend. He'd grown up in a little town outside of Syracuse and was studying at Albany now for a career in administration of something or other. Anyway, he knew how it was with me and that professor jerk, and he'd heard about this latest turn of events and hoped a punch was the wake-up call I needed, but for now he was just making sure I was okay. He sat by my bed as "Tuesday Afternoon" played over and over, and he

46

offered me orange juice and put an extra blanket over me as the room grew dark and drafty, and he stroked my head and stayed with me, and I closed my eyes and drifted. Hours passed.

This happened too: Right before he left the room, believing I was fast asleep, Jack leaned forward and kissed me on the forehead.

It was the tender gesture of a parent, almost. It was innocent and gentle, secret and spontaneous, not made for response or observation. It was decent and kind and quietly bestowed, the sort of behavior that had lately been so lacking in my life, I had forgotten it was normal.

So something did call to me and draw me near on this Tuesday long ago. I woke up feeling valued. Simple as that. A little bit better, subtly changed.

Neither vigil nor kiss was ever mentioned. Jack was just someone I knew, and I was a confused young woman, slowly and painfully inching my way forward with plenty of big mistakes still ahead. And yet.

I was beginning to see.

PART II

A BLUR

Well I'm gonna get through this world
The best I can, if I can
  – Woody Guthrie, from "Gonna Get Through This World"

49

13

TEACHING

I began my teaching career at the age of forty-three. I was still grieving over the recent death of my brother Eddie, and I wanted to do something constructive and hopeful in his memory. I viewed teaching as a noble calling – perhaps because I was lucky enough to have had one or two teachers in my own life who had filled me with a sense of possibility.

I thought of my eleventh-grade history teacher, Mr. Sexton, a man as often the object of furtive derision as grudging respect. Like all school teachers, he possessed eccentricities of behavior and appearance which generated cruel nicknames and set him apart from normal human beings – but this was standard. One rainy day in June of 1967, he brought out a record player and had us listen to "The Impossible Dream" from *Man of La Mancha*, which at the time was a Broadway hit. As the music played, we silently read the lyrics from the purple-inked mimeographed sheets he had distributed.

At one point I looked up and saw that Mr. Sexton had tears in his eyes. It was embarrassing – it cut too close. I knew that he saw this song as an inspiring creed by which to live our lives; its lyrics were his gift to us, a parting message. But I did not wish to contemplate Mr. Sexton's personal dreams and vulnerability, nor could I ever admit that this schmaltz affected me, as well. I lowered my gaze and never said a word. But I never forgot it, either.

Thirty years later, as a middle school teacher myself, I knew very well how Mr. Sexton must have felt alone in his classroom after the bell. There were many days when I simply didn't think I was getting through, no matter how much I gave. Just as it was in 1967, the facade of coolness seemed to be the ubiquitous mask of adolescence. And one of the things a teacher has to learn is that you don't always know who you are reaching, or even when the message will arrive. But you must keep trying – for you are the knight of the impossible dream, and shining idealism must be your armor.

Even when we do not feel brave or hopeful, those of us who are teachers, or parents, for that matter, are morally obligated to act in brave and hopeful ways. If our house is flooded, and all that we possess is a thimble, then thimble by thimble we must begin to empty the water. We must demonstrate our own conviction that in time the task will be accomplished, and we must prove our willingness to labor towards that end. What's more, we must show those within our reach how to cup their hands and help.

I will be honest. Sometimes I looked at students, particularly as a new teacher, and asked myself who these aliens were. Maybe it came of starting a career in middle age. For my entire first year, I wondered what had become of discipline and respect. I yearned to foster constructive social action. I was troubled by self-centered rudeness and indifference to the pain of others. "They're only kids," people told me. "You have to meet them on their own terms."

For a time, I accepted this. But eventually I came to my senses. Their terms? Will the world meet them on their terms? Are there not values and rules of conduct that they must adopt? I realized it was up to me to model responsible adult behavior, hold kids accountable for their actions, and broaden their sphere of awareness. Particularly among middle school students, who wander in that strange border country called adolescence, a sense of moral direction is essential, but it isn't implicitly learned through the basic curriculum. I found a like-minded colleague, Jennifer Levin, and we set out on a mission.

Teaching is an act of supreme defiance against apathy and cynicism, and to strip it of its moral component is to render it without a soul. At the beginning of school, Jennifer and I took our class to the Museum of Tolerance in Los Angeles. Students were confronted with images and voices of the Holocaust, a time not so far removed from the present. "Evil persists when good people do nothing." We saw what evil looks like, what indifference sustains. It was quite a jolt.

But we cannot simply get depressed about it. Depression is self-indulgent. One must use the fuel of sadness and anger to build a fire that warms. We required our students to find tangible ways to make the world a better place. They visited homeless children, collected canned goods, raised money for Habitat for Humanity. They learned that they each have the power to mitigate the world's collective misery, rather than adding to it.

Because of the nature of our world, it was all too easy to find examples of intolerance and suffering throughout the social studies curriculum. We also looked for the people in history who stood up for what was right. Students wrote about times in their own lives when they had done the right thing. They created children's books with moral themes. I found that moral courage is a concept that students had not consciously explored, nor is it a principle that can simply be preached. Moral courage and decency must be modeled by the significant adults in a child's life. Teachers must be particularly aware of the behaviors they demonstrate, whether it means containing anger or giving it a righteous voice.

Jennifer and I also emphasized the small civilities that make life more pleasant. We taught manners, using sometimes comical role-playing, and culminating in an "etiquette dinner" in which our classroom was transformed into an elegant restaurant. Students learned that the purpose of manners is to make people more comfortable. "It hurts my feelings when you walk in and don't say good morning to me," I confessed. I was no longer invisible. They humored me, at least.

I stealthily monitored many interactions outside of the classroom, as well. "You have no right to butt in!" said one indignant student. But I decided that butting in is a teacher's duty, too. One cannot teach character if one is bent on being popular or cool. I called kids on meanness, tactlessness, even just plain old foul language, which I simply feel loses its power from overuse, and is a flaccid and uncreative way to express oneself.

We often took the pathway of poetry, for it leads directly to the heart. The students wrote poems about their adolescent pain, Jennifer and I dug up some awful poetry we ourselves had written, and we sat in a circle on the floor and shared these. We could empathize with one another, be a little gentler, perhaps.

I thought it was a good start, but Jennifer and I drew up student questionnaires to help us assess the impact. The first part consisted of a series of hypothetical situations in which students were asked to write down what they should do, and what they actually would do. Some responses were inadvertently funny:

Your friend asks if he can copy your homework. What would you do?

I would normely say I did not do it nether.

Someone at school is always sitting alone at lunch. What would you do?

I would probably ignore him too but I would feel sorry for him.

Many replies revealed that students would not necessarily do what they knew they should do, and I was disappointed at first, but then felt gratitude for their honesty. In fact, their answers indicated that they were thinking about each situation, that they were at least aware of values and moral principles upon which to base their reactions, and finally, that they were not going to simply snow their teachers with the answers they thought we wanted. I saw this as a good thing.

Besides, these kids didn't know what would and would not affect them, any more than I knew in 1967 that I would someday be influenced by Mr. Sexton's tears. I believe in the retroactive nature of learning. Seeds I planted may lie dormant for years, then flower unexpectedly in the rain and sun of the future.

In the second part of the questionnaire, students wrote an open-ended essay about how the class had changed them, if at all. Almost everyone mentioned pride about having done community service, a greater awareness of prejudice and intolerance, and the fact that they now treated people with more politeness. No one waxed poetic, no one claimed that their lives had been significantly altered, no one was inspired to change the world... or even become a teacher. A few admitted they did not really know what the effect of all this had been. And one student wrote, "I did not get anything out of this class because the teachers did not seem to realize that this is reality and we can't become color blind with the flick of a switch..." He's the one who convinced me to keep going.

Notice how I have turned negatives into positives. I ignored all the reasons to stop and found only reasons to continue. I believed in the hope, even when it was a lie. I taught because although I knew that "this is reality", I will never accept that it must be so, and I found it particularly unacceptable that a thirteen-year-old boy did. I went forth to battle windmills, injustice, or simply ennui. To teach was to head a revolution every day.

14

MANATEE

It is the day after Thanksgiving and we have gathered on a wooden pier at the Indian River near Palm Bay, Florida in the hopes of seeing a manatee. We are family and strangers, children and grown-ups, Southern drawls and New York City accents. Little Rose gets down on her belly, dips her hands, and gently splashes. She is wearing pink as usual and has no idea what a manatee is, but she is fully caught up in the excitement of finding out. Sunlight paints the muddy water, every bubble and shimmer draws our rapt attention, and it feels as though we are on a small raft together – a raft of fools, perhaps, but cheerful ones. In a Walmart three miles away, shoppers are scrambling for merchandise in the avaricious frenzy of holiday shopping officially uncorked this very morning and I feel a bond with those who have the sense to be here instead. The day is an island of green and blue, heartbreaking in its loveliness.

Strange, ungainly creatures, the manatees are migratory aquatic mammals that find their way to the warm shallow waters of slow-moving rivers, estuaries, saltwater bays, canals and coastal areas. They are gentle half-ton herbivores constantly grazing for food along the bottoms and surfaces of the water, hence their nickname: sea cows. Manatees have no natural enemies and can live for sixty years if they avoid encounters with boat propellers or other human-caused dangers. Sailors of long ago mistook them for mermaids, but these men must have been at sea too long – it is hard to imagine a homelier animal.

We have come to this place like pilgrims hoping for a glimpse, and our patience is rewarded. First, bubbles appear, and a glimmering mirage just beneath the surface of the water. Next a curious pair of nostrils makes a shy appearance, and when at last a wrinkled whiskered snout emerges, we all gasp in wonderment. Silent and trusting, the manatees draw nearer to us, even accepting the touch of our hands. I am inexplicably happy to reach beyond my human-ness and defer to the dignity of this elephantine emissary from the natural world. It is comforting to know that there are manatees.

Comfort comes when you least expect it. It would be an understatement to say I had been worried about this Florida trip. More accurately, I was terrified. For one thing, it would be my first trip back since the death of my sister. I dreaded the sight of the familiar house where she no longer waited. I didn't want to stand in her kitchen trying to remember the sound of her voice. And then there was the whole prospect of meeting up with family. Family: the ones who know you too well, the ones who know you least. Since our current lives don't overlap, we tend to dwell on the history we've shared, and my family's history just isn't any fun. I knew of course we would try to be cheery. Then all the old pain would press upon our hearts, and all the old angers would spark and collide; regressive dynamics would kick into place, and I would be crazy again. But I have sailed across 3,000 miles of sky to take my place among this ragtag assemblage. I guess this is what people do.

There is an oak tree by her grave with Spanish moss and wind chimes in its branches. Her name on a stone stuns me for a second but the sense of loss is neither deepened nor dulled. My sadness is a cold, familiar wind through a broken pane – and this too is what it feels like to be human. I am afraid I learn almost everything a little bit too late, but for now I let myself close my eyes and think about forgiveness. I hear a sparkling sound like jewels in the air and try to fill myself with light. I cast away regrets and imagine them flickering like aspen leaves, like shiny coins that jingle like the wind chimes in the tree.

And I am absorbed into the dominion of the present, where miracles are unfolding all around me. Every day could be a hymn of gratitude. The water sparkles in the sunlight, the air is rich with river, and good-hearted people take time out for inter-species communion. Now the Dixie Chicks are singing on the radio, the menu at Dot's includes salsa and grits, and Rose is drawing pictures at the table. It isn't helpful to torment ourselves for what happened years ago. We are all flawed and short-lived; we may as well ease up and stand still for a moment and listen to something other than our own tired voices.

Trust me on this. I am someone who has seen a manatee.

15

ENGLAND

We were walking along a narrow street lined with brick row houses topped by chimneys, past an old pub and a bright red postal box, everything around us so other than the way it is at home. Even the grocery stores intrigued me, stocked as they are with different kinds of chocolate and cereal and yogurt, fruit weighed out in kilograms, heaps of pale root vegetables. The oatmeal was called porridge. There was piccalilli, and clotted cream, and small brown jars of Marmite.

"I love coming here!" I exclaimed.

"Words never before uttered, ever, by anyone, upon entering Tesco," said my daughter.

Nothing seemed ordinary, especially not the cinematic clouds, and fields of white dandelions ready to be wished on, and the damp smell of mud and nettles by the river. Little children spoke in Peter Pan accents, a fellow cycled by carrying a drum, and the white light of evening lingered eerily late.

"We're strolling around in England! Can you even believe you live here?" I asked my daughter. "Don't you find yourself in a constant state of astonishment? Or are you just so over it?"

"Can't I be something midway between astonished and jaded?" she said. "Why are those two extremes my only options?"

And therein perhaps lies the crux of my own problem. I veer around continually from wonder to despair. It's exhausting. I shall strive for quiet equanimity today.

16

TIME IS A COUNTRY

Miranda and I are taking the train from Oxford to Bath for a mother-daughter weekend before I go back home to California. We have chosen Bath on the basis of simplicity: it's a short, easy trip, a manageable place, and a good setting in which to talk and relax. "It's where Women of a Certain Age go to be pampered," adds her boyfriend, and I can't say if this appeals to me.

But there seems to be more shopping than pampering taking place in Bath, and my daughter and I will do a bit of that ourselves, stopping into bookstores and dress shops as we wander through the city, along the Royal Crescent, Parade Road, Cheap Street. We walk by the River Avon, through beautiful parks, past well-tended gardens and stately Georgian buildings. There are young mothers pushing strollers through the park, dads with babies on their shoulders, tattooed teenagers talking on cell phones, weighty matrons licking ice cream cones and trying on sensible shoes.

First, though, we check into a bed and breakfast on a quiet street across from the park. It is run by a German woman named Inge who leads us upstairs to a pale green room overlooking a garden. There are twin beds, side by side, with a little lamp next to each, and it feels exactly right. We have come here to reconnect, to catch up, to get to know each other as we are.

In the evening we have dinner with a friend of Miranda's from school and her mother, V., who live in Bath. The daughters engage in animated conversation about their writing and their lives, and we mothers seem to know each other immediately. Both of us are still in a state of astonishment at how fast everything has happened, but as we watch our girls sail off into lives of their own, we are also hoping there is time for us to claim some small adventure for ourselves. V. has a chance to live for a year in Kenya, a prospect she finds both intriguing and daunting. She is disenchanted with her English life and ready for something new.

"It's hard to find happy people here," says her daughter, who is planning a summer adventure involving a boyfriend, a motorcycle, and a continent or two.

As Miranda and I walk back to the guest house it seems the streets are filled with drunken carousers. One unappealing fellow is parading around with pants that open in the back to reveal his ass to all the world, and many of the girls are dressed like hookers in short, skin-tight skirts and precariously high heels, but there are also loud, laughing women in complicated hats and glitzy Saturday night costumes. It is a procession of the badly dressed.

"How is your writing going?" Miranda asks me. She is a writer herself, and a good one. In response, I hear myself using words like deflated. I talk about being in a lull, about maybe just trying to make my life be my art. I don't know anymore if I will ever do any serious writing.

"Well, you are in your sixties," she says, not unkindly. "It's not the same, is it?"

I suppose it's not.

A pair of hot air balloons cruise lazily in the air high above the rooftops and steeples. We walk through a park, now emptied of people, where vacant blue and white striped chairs are clustered in circles as if having a party of their own. When we return to our room, it is still illuminated by the lingering white light of this first night of summer.

My daughter loves her life. "If it helps to know this," she says, "I have never been happier." It does help.

The next day I buy her earrings, silver ballet flats from a charity store, and a book by an Irish poet she likes named Louis MacNeice, whose work I have never read, but he is wonderful. I open it at random: *Time is a country, the present moment/a spotlight roving round the scene.*

On our last morning in Bath, we chat for a bit with Inge, who turns to Miranda as we leave and says, "Take good care of your mom."

It's an innocent comment, but it makes me wonder if I am someone who seems in need of care, and I ponder this as we walk to the station. I worry sometimes about becoming one of those baffled and befuddled types who's in everybody's way. But for now, I am feeling self-contained and unafraid, hoping there might still be one good stretch ahead.

And I came here not to be pampered but to pause, just to pause and focus on this interesting young woman who five minutes ago was a streak of color running through my house. I take her hand as we walk through a very green park smelling roses and grass.

A little girl in a red dress pedals by on a bicycle giggling.

17

A BRIGHTNESS

This is the way grief is: You walk along feeling reasonably engaged in the present, looking at things, just being in the world… and then something terribly sad appears in your head and you're suddenly not here anymore. You feel that if you tried to talk, it would just come out in sobs, and you certainly don't want to unleash all of that, so you stay quiet and wait for it to pass. And it does pass, until the next time.

On this particular day we were in Brighton, an old coastal town in East Sussex. Our primary mission was to visit a woman who sells vintage wedding dresses, but it was also a pleasant expedition, and we conveniently still had our rental car. We had a leisurely drive and arrived around lunchtime. We sat by the steamy window of a little café watching the motley procession of tourists and locals hurrying by, and the song "Sugar Man" was playing, and there were aromas of hot tea and roasted butternut squash and bread fresh from the oven. There was a comforting murmur of conversation, and a clarity of color and light and beautiful prosaic life.

"Everything is so intense," I said.

Monte looked at me skeptically, maybe a little worried. "Isn't that what people used to say after they dropped acid?"

"But that's not how I mean it," I said. "It's just..."

And I couldn't really explain. Life comes over me in waves sometimes, bringing with it a fusion of heartache and wonder that almost leaves me gasping. There's so much to take in, so much to appreciate, so much to bear, so much to reconcile and fathom and accept.

We walked along the waterfront, a pebbled beach, nearly deserted, empty benches facing the sea, the charred remnants of a Victorian pier in the distance. There were even a few stand-up paddle boarders out there, reminding us of home.

Then we found our way to the wedding dress lady, and I watched my daughter try on dresses, each with a story of its own, and she was lovely and hopeful, and I sat squarely in the moment, from whence I looked forward instead of back.

18

RECORDS

They had come to the Ranch years ago, but they were moving on and clearing out the house. They decided to have a garage sale to get rid of the last few remnants and they put announcements in all the mailboxes, but it was mostly an excuse to get together with friends and toast an era's end. They stood on the deck greeting people, and they set out shrimps and cocktail sauce, sour cream and onion dip beside a bowl heaped with chips, and several bottles of wine. I wish I had been wearing a silk caftan in a bright paisley print.

The interior of the house was sunlit and almost bare, with a few faded prints on the walls, a stray piece of furniture here and there, and an enormous elk head above the stairs waiting for a new owner. In a shadowy corner to the left of the staircase was the record collection, all of it up for grabs, and I was drawn to it immediately.

Truth is, I don't even own a record player, but I wasn't planning to shop. I just wanted to enjoy the pleasure of perusal. And I perused with tenderness, for as I scrolled through the albums, it was clear to me that I was leafing through the history of a family, an audio documentation of the time in which they lived, and the soundtrack of their lives in varied epochs.

I came first upon an album – and here I mean album literally, the kind that is a hard-covered book and in between are pages holding separate 78s – of *Big Ten College Songs*. Underneath that, there was a Victor Musical Masterpiece collection entitled *Negro Spirituals Sung by Dorothy Maynor with Unaccompanied Male Choir*. Okay, I admit it: I had to own the latter, and I bought it for three dollars. Who could have resisted classics like "Go Tell It on the Mountain" or "Nobody Knows the Trouble I've Seen" sung by a soprano whose voice was once described (by Boston Symphony conductor Serge Koussevitzky) as a miracle and a musical revelation? Tucked inside there was even an added bonus: a record of Marian Anderson singing "Deep River" and "Dere's No Hiding Place Down Dere".

There were lots of LPs, of course, in random profusion: symphonies by Mahler, Mozart, and Tchaikovsky, Scott Joplin tunes played by the New England Conservatory Ragtime Ensemble, piano hits of Roger Williams, ballads sung by Burl Ives, and the same Broadway musicals I listened to as a kid, with covers as familiar as old friends. One glimpse of Mary Martin and Ezio Pinza on the cover of *South Pacific*, and I was hearing "Some Enchanted Evening" in my head. A glance at Mario Lanza on *The Student Prince*, and his dulcet tenor tones were serenading me about moonbeams and dreaming and I could drift along forever, and yes, this is the stuff that was playing in my house while I was growing up. Especially eerie was the sight of *Whistle While You Work: Music with a Lilt to Lighten Your Housework* and its whimsical illustration of a woman circa 1961 in a striped dress and white apron with a schmata on her head, dancing jubilantly with a broom. We owned this record too. Did everyone?

There was a kids' corner as well: *The Chipmunks Sing Again, Bozo on the Farm, Songs of the Wild West,* and *Fire Station Songs* with a twenty-nine-cent price tag still on the paper jacket. I skipped a group of 45s and wandered over to the talking LPs of the early sixties. We all remember The *First Family* by Vaughn Meader, when Camelot was spoof-able. Here too was Tom Lehrer's *That Was the Year That Was,* and Mort Sahl, *Look Forward in Anger.* These were the artifacts of our youth and shared history.

It was a time capsule, that's what it was, and oddly poignant, as garage sales always are. And the lady of the house came up to me and sweetly said, "Just take them all. I want you to have them."

I held the collection of spirituals with tenderness but declined the rest. It wasn't just that I couldn't play them anyway. Or that Monte would be furious if I came home with three or four big boxes filled with stuff, whether old or new. It wasn't even the unexpected lump in my throat. It was just a very strong sense of already having more than enough.

The following Monday, I brought my newly purchased records with me to school, knowing there were kindred spirits among my colleagues who appreciated this sort of thing. I carried them over to the redwood picnic table where folks were standing around during recess.

"Hang on a minute," said the science teacher, Treebeard, and he hurried off to his classroom. He came back schlepping an old-fashioned Victrola phonograph, the kind with a wind-up crank arm and an internal amplifying horn built into a heavy wooden case.

Now honestly, what are the odds?

He lifted a record from its envelope, set it on the turntable, wound up the lever, and gently placed the needle in a groove.

Suddenly Marian Anderson was singing "Deep River" as we gathered in the sunshine by a picnic table, seventy years after the recording was made. The kids grew silent; everyone stood listening. The scratches and pops somehow added to the magic.

We were all a bit late for class.

19

HEIRESS

Yesterday I faced the difficult task of clearing out my mother's room. Her familiar clothes were hanging in the closet, and I knew which were her favorites and the provenance of each. The drawers were brimming with beads and broken watches, eyeglasses and trinkets, fancy fans and shoe horns, random treasures neatly wrapped and taped in tissue paper: a screw, a domino, a broken piece of star. I saw the dolls whose names were Darling and Miranda, and good old Betty Boop, and the steadfast white bear with the heart on his chest who sat on the bed pillow through many hard times. Now they were gathered together like orphaned children awaiting their destiny.

I approached it all in a trance-like state, turning off my emotions so I wouldn't start to cry. Thankfully I was accompanied by my dear friend Donna, who was functional and clear-thinking. A sorting system evolved, with bags for the Goodwill, for the dumpster out back, and smallest of all, for stuff to be kept. "Take your time," said Donna, more than once, holding up some item of potential value, whether real or sentimental. "Are you sure this isn't something you'll wish you'd held onto?" But I was ruthless in the giving and the throwing away. I didn't want things that I knew would only make me sad.

So many hair ties and barrettes, so many chapsticks and lipsticks, so many unwrapped butterscotch candies. So many pens and crayons, and letters and cards almost all sent by me, so many handkerchiefs and scissors and post-it notes and magazine clippings and little mirrors and napkins and pictures of kittens and brochures with smiling people on the covers. So many books with handwritten notes tucked into them, so many purses and keys to nowhere, so many emery boards and band-aids and a secret stash of hearing aid batteries. Money, too: a long-forgotten dollar bill folded into a tiny pink coin purse, and about seventy-nine cents worth of change.

And everywhere there were photographs of people she loved, and of course they're the same ones I loved, the original cast of characters. She and I sat side by side many times going through these albums and looking at those snapshots, and she never forgot who they were. Just weeks before she died, I showed her the framed picture of my father, and she leaned forward and kissed it. I've taken those photographs with me.

I also took the composition notebooks we referred to as our journals. These were a ritual: at the conclusion of each visit over the years, I would open to a fresh page and write the date and what we did together. I thought it would help her stay oriented and allow her to revisit the memories. They are thus a record of our outings over the course of fifteen years, with the diminishing radius of our expeditions reflecting her diminishing capabilities. They also document her accumulating problems, filled as they are with reminders, advice, and attempts at reassurance. So I've inherited the journals, and I'll read them, I guess, but I don't think I'll keep them. I remember enough.

The mezuzah is mine as well. It was mounted on the wall by the door, and she always touched it before passing the threshold. "Heaven keep our going and coming each day." It's a kind of blessing and protection, and I like that it was hers. I've hung it by the door in the upstairs room of my house, a threshold of some importance to me. It reminds me to stay faithful to what matters.

Life moves along too fast too fast but after a while we look back and see what wasn't clear to us while everything was happening. I understand now that my mother's childlike enthusiasm was something rare and beautiful, and I can see how very brave she was. I am in awe of her resilience and stamina. She weathered terrible loss and loneliness and traumatic upheavals, but she remembered mostly good things and tried to be game. Discarding the remnants of face powders and blushers, I recall how much she liked to look pretty, and I remember how surprised she was to be old. And I realize in retrospect how much she loved music... in the deafness of her final decade she missed it more and more, and she hummed to herself a lot. I see again how fond she was of animals, and I wish she could have had a real pet in these years, but she was always on the lookout for a cat slinking by on the street or a bird splashing in the patio fountain. I must never forget how the simplest of pleasures can brighten someone's day.

And I marvel at how much she loved to go outside and walk. Even after she fell and broke her hip, she swapped her cane for a walker and kept on moving. Here's a quote from her, age eighty-nine, that I jotted down in one of the journals: "Eighty-nine. It's pretty old... isn't it? But I don't feel my age. I could still run... if I ever have to run, I could run." Yes, my mother thought of herself as someone who could still run if she had to. She hated that wheelchair, another object left behind, but not one we ever really thought of as hers.

It's a pretty good legacy, after all. I don't know if I could ever be as stoic and brave as she was, but maybe after I get up and pull myself together, I'll discover that I've inherited some of her resilience and stamina. I'll definitely be inspired by her enthusiasm. And I already know I find great comfort in mobility, which I'm sure is a gift from her. (Some of my earliest memories, come to think of it, involve walking all over the city with her, she in high heels.)

Most important, I have had an excellent internship in patience, and I've been bequeathed a small trove of wisdom. I have learned that you only end up regretting the times you were unkind, and that what you perceived as a burden may turn out to have been a gift. And I'm not going to be sad, damn it. I'm going to try, as my mother did, to remember what was good.

So we cleared the room of my mother's worldly goods, and a poignant collection it was. Ninety-one years of living, and this is what she owned. People have asked me if I am the executor of my mother's estate, and I never thought about it that way, but yes, I suppose I am. Not only that, I'm an heiress.

20

A FRONT

A front moved in… a wall of white cloud and cold air that seemed to alter everything. The light was tinged with blue, and dim, like a too-soon dusk, and the hills looked frosty, and everything felt strange.

Everything *is* strange… isn't it? *The route has been recalculated. Please drive onto a digitized road.* But where? I can't see past the front.

I used to pray at night, an earnest hybrid of a prayer, and one of the things I used to say was, "Let me be an instrument of love and light."

I don't even know what that means. These are ugly, disillusioning times.

I liked being out of the country for a while. When I was far away, what is happening to our democracy was easier to mute. We're living with an illness now, a collective trauma, a debilitating daily onslaught. I know we need to act, but sometimes I feel helpless.

A friend of mine tells me that my writing is always sad. But I think I'm just being honest, trying to write through to some sort of sense, to that band of light behind the clouds.

A month ago, I was in Paris. I was walking along a street in Paris called Rue de Turbigo, and suddenly, completely out of context, I remembered my mother looking up at me from her bed not long before her death, and she could hardly speak, but she mouthed the words, "I love you so much."

Oh, those sudden flashbacks... they bring an almost physical pain.

Did I say, "I love you so much" back? I honestly can't remember. And would saying it have mattered? It's as if I was in some kind of trance. There are so many things I wish I had said, and so many questions I wish I had asked, so many things I wish we had talked about over the years.

(I wonder if my daughter will feel this about me someday.)

But I said the words out loud in Paris on Rue de Turbigo. I said it to the air: "I love you so much."

My voice blended with the traffic and noise and cacophony of the city. It radiated outward and floated upward and dissolved into sound waves and molecules moving through time.

I am putting up a brave front.

21

ALMOST

Nothing had changed except that a particular possibility had ended. It was just a little flicker of a possibility and it had not progressed very far, and from this there were no terrible repercussions, just a tiny gasp of loss, a pause, an altered course. We'd held onto the delicious secret for several weeks. We were going to be grandparents. And then suddenly we were not, as simple as that. There were wisps of clouds in the sky that day, an autumnal slant of light, the air like a sigh.

My sense of bereavement for what almost was but never came to be seemed irrational, disproportionate – and yet it could not be denied. A sweet promise had been bestowed upon us, and we had been savoring it. We anticipated and imagined and even assumed, and I thought about how this birth would bring our life full circle, how a little time traveler would pivot us around to a forward perspective. And now it was gone, having barely begun.

But mostly I was sad for our daughter. I wanted, and still want, for her to know the joy of becoming a mother, because being her mother was the happiest part of my life.

Miscarriage. I hate the word. It implies a mistake, fault, carelessness, a baby pram toppled over or rolling away out of reach. And as it turns out, my daughter was to experience subsequent miscarriages; this was only the first. Her doctor told her that miscarriage in early pregnancy was common, and that in most cases, when it happens, it is unavoidable, the result of chromosomal abnormalities that would have made the embryo unviable anyway. But there is scant comfort in this.

Our daughter described it this way: "One morning I woke up and felt, it's strange to say, like *myself* again – not weary, not queasy – and that evening I experienced mild pain, a quick gush of blood which soon slowed to a trickle, and a sense of foreboding."

Maybe it's nothing, her husband said. You don't know yet.

But it was something. She knew.

And at the edges of her sadness, she felt almost a sense of relief, because the dreaded thing had happened, and all of her worrying, which could control nothing anyway, could cease.

She has endured it with courage and dignity, but I am certain it's more painful and disappointing than I can even imagine.

"Now everything is different," she writes, "and everything will be different again someday, and different again, and different again. How much of this I can directly influence I do not know: the body demands active ownership and management, but it also disobeys and disregards, decays, betrays."

It is dangerous to want something so much over which one has no control.

But it's impossible not to want.

"There needs to be something else in our lives," she said one day when I tried to talk about it. It's true of course, but I can picture her and her husband telling each other things like this in the middle of the night, bracing themselves, uttering such words as a buffer against disappointment. And they *do* have other things in their lives.

All around her, though, people are having babies. She's too decent to begrudge others their joy or to perceive their happiness as somehow diminishing her own, but I imagine there is wistfulness or envy, and a sadness at the core.

In any case, *I* admit to it.

It's random and cruel, and there is nothing to be done.

But the world offers sufficient distractions, and the days proceed, and when I talk to our faraway daughter, my heart experiences what can only be described as a brimming over of love. I would protect her from all hurt if only I could.

I cherish beginnings, nonetheless, however they conclude. Those feelings were real, and I felt them, and I remember how it was.

And maybe if we walk the detours with courage and love, we can see with clarity how much is still here.

When I began to write, I thought this was about loss, but it has somehow become about finding. I have been telling myself something, and I will say it aloud to you now on the page:

Do not let the forces of the world unravel all your hopes, and if they do, re-stitch and reshape. Make of them a shawl, not a shroud, something of beauty, knit loose enough to let in light, snug enough for warmth, surprisingly resilient.

PART III

I FIND MYSELF
HERE

Will you ever bring a better gift for the world
than the breathing respect that you carry
wherever you go right now? Are you waiting
for time to show you some better thoughts?
   – William Stafford, from "You Reading This, Be Ready"

22

SIX TREES

1

When I was in grade school, one of my most memorable home-work assignments was to choose a tree and watch it over time. We were to draw a picture of it in a notebook, observe bark, branch, and leaf, note seasonal changes, and describe clearly. What kind of tree was it? Could we estimate its height, or the circumference of its trunk? Did birds or squirrels find a welcome in it? Were there sounds if we listened, smells if we sniffed? It was, in retrospect, a high-quality lesson in science, language arts, and observation. And especially in view of the fact that we were living in the thick of urban Brooklyn, it was a wise teacher who guided us to focus on nature.

I believe my tree was a maple, and it was a very young tree then. I remember its general location and even went back and looked for it once, fifty years later, but I couldn't recognize it. There are maples here and there. Who knows? One of them might even be mine.

Thanks to all teachers who point city kids to trees and to the nat-ural world still thriving at the edges of things, and sometimes in the midst. I'm worried about the planet these days, as I'm sure all enlightened humans are, but it occurs to me that unless children are taught to notice and appreciate the natural environment, they won't know what we stand to lose.

2

I used to have occasional chats with Tony Ochoa, who grew up on this ranch during the 1920s and 30s. I liked to check in with him to see how he was doing, but I also just enjoyed hearing stories about his childhood here. One day I mentioned that I think of him whenever I drive past the palm tree he planted in 1934. (Tony passed away a few years ago, and I *still* think of him when I see his tree.)

"You know, I was only nine years old when I planted that tree," said Tony, "and I can't imagine why it was so important to me. I had tried others before it, and I learned a lot each time. I found that one when it was a little four-inch seedling at Bulito Canyon. I soaked it real good, and then I took a coffee can with the bottom removed, put it around the seedling, and pressed hard to drive the can down through the mud. I was able to lift the seedling out, roots intact within the can, and I carried it over and planted it where it is now."

"Doesn't that seem funny for a nine-year-old boy?" he asked me. "I look at my nine-year-old grandson today, and it's hard to imagine him taking all that trouble to plant a tree, being so serious about it, so determined. But that was my world, I guess, and that was how I learned."

"Outdoor education," I suggested.

"I suppose. And they used to have round-ups over there at Gaviota," he continued. "The horses were stomping around, and my little tree was taking a beating. I asked the railroad foreman to drop off some railroad ties. I dragged them over with my horse, and then I put them in the ground around the tree to form a barrier to protect it. Nine years old. I wonder why I cared so much about that tree."

"Well, Tony," I said, "I guess it was your project. And the tree is still there. You may have been a little boy, but there's something very hopeful about planting a tree. You sent a gift into the future."

Then we talked some more about old times in this part of the world, and as I always do when I hear the stories or read about the past, I felt I a deeper connection to this place, and a deeper appreciation.

I had called Tony to see if he was okay, but afterwards I realized it was to help *me* be okay.

Tree-planting tales are especially welcome. Stories of things that survive. Constructive efforts and small hopeful gestures. I need those.

3

Jeanne calls it the lion oak because once at dusk when she was driving up the road she saw a mountain lion on one of its thick lower limbs. But the tree is a lion in its own right too: a magnificent being, a king in our canyon, a silent sentinel to a passing century or two.

When my daughter was a little girl, the lion oak served as a prop for a math assignment. She estimated its height by comparing shadow lengths, measured the circumference of its massive trunk with an insufficient tape measure, carefully avoiding the poison oak on the side nearest the creek, and put her arms around it afterwards as far as they could go just to feel its solidity and strength. I can still picture her there when I pass that tree, a small brown-haired child, a little bit wild, a girl who felt at home here.

My daughter of course is far away, but the trusty old tree still stands. One night on an impulse we took a walk with friends to see it. The moon peered through its branches, waxing poetic, lovesick and loathe to leave. Indeed, many love and have loved the old lion oak, but it belongs to itself.

The tree reveals itself differently depending on the light or the mindset of the viewer. On this night its bark looked gray and scarred and vulnerable up close, and some of us were sad, absorbing losses in our personal lives, horrified by a mass shooting that had happened in our country on that particular day, dismayed by the political scene and wanting so much to believe that our nation is better than that spectacle.

But we also felt an unequivocal sense of wonder and reassurance in the presence of the tree. And you might have laughed to see us standing there, looking up at that old tree, four gray-haired people, endlessly fascinated. The soundtrack was frog song and the rustle of leaves.

4

My mother stood by the open screened window of her room in the assisted living facility and pointed excitedly to the top of a tall, leafy tree visible just beyond the rooftop of an adjacent building, and said (in her *loud* voice, with its New York accent): "See that tree, Cynthia? That gorgeous tree? It's my favorite tree! It's the most beautiful tree in the world!"

A couple of guys were on a patio just a few feet from the window – they were workers of some sort, taking a break, talking in Spanish – and of course my mother had to bring them into the experience. "Hello!" she called out to them, as though they were old friends. (And *loudly*, yes.) Next, she had to introduce me, simply because she introduced me to everyone, whether or not they had met me before, and these men most assuredly had not: "This is my daughter Cynthia! She's here visiting me!"

Finally, most important, she informed the men that they were within sight of her favorite tree. "Right over there… see? *It's the most beautiful tree in the world!*" I think she fully expected them to share in her excitement. They nodded and smiled wanly. Crazy old lady at the window. One of them half-turned to sort of glance at the tree.

It was time to go. I gave her some lip balm, a coloring book and crayons, and a butterscotch sucker from Mrs. See's. I turned her TV set onto a show with captions for the hearing impaired. Then I said good-bye and retreated to the refuge of my own life. My friend Vickie asked me if the trip was depressing. Well, let's say it was a tall glass of depressing with a shot of profound sadness and a twist of dismay.

But you know? It occurred to me afterwards that we had indeed been looking at the most beautiful tree in the world. Because there it was: a reliable presence, its lofty crown of green a familiar and comforting sight, its grandeur the constant opposite of everything ugly and mundane. The most beautiful tree in the world is the one that you can see.

5

My mother-in-law plants trees. I love that about her. She propagates oaks and sycamores. She grows citrus, avocado, and macadamia trees, and a garden of native plants. She tends to things.

The other day as I was walking past the orchard, she asked me if I would like a grapefruit. "Of course," I said. She handed me a couple. They had heft.

"You realize you can pick these any time," she said. I don't know why I don't. Whenever I taste them, tart, and refreshing, and utterly delicious, I realize they're exactly what I've been craving.

She stepped back and looked up at the tree with satisfaction, even a bit of pride. She's a tiny, white-haired lady, ninety years old, in a baseball cap and sneakers.

"That's my best tree," she said.

I noticed it as though for the first time. It's astonishingly leafy and green and symmetrical, reaching out wide from its small sturdy trunk, and almost always laden with fruit. It's luckily positioned in terms of soil and water, even in these days of stress and drought. It *is* a handsome tree. Productive, too.

Sometimes I take so much for granted. I walk by wonders without a second thought. Yes, my mother-in-law plants trees, and it's one of the things I love about her. I didn't even know she had favorites.

6

We had a pine tree growing near our house for nearly twenty years. I was used to seeing it through the bedroom window bathed in the light of new morning, and now and then, at the cusp of night, with a pale moon hanging over it. I liked watching birds fly toward it to take shelter in its branches, and I liked the way the wind trembled its needles. I liked the cooling shadows it cast, and I liked its piney fragrance. It was very much there. In a good way.

The pine tree had been planted in the sandy dirt of a steep hillside, and it grew first at an angle and then straight up, taller and faster than we expected, and the rock beneath the surface of the hillside prevented its roots from gripping deeply. Occasionally we wondered what would happen if it fell; it was very close to the house. But mostly we didn't think about it. It was just there. In a good way.

Then came the fire, and all our vulnerabilities were exacerbated. Everyone has been clearing dry brush, cutting away dead tree limbs, removing trees that might easily catch fire, opening pathways, creating fire breaks. We looked up at the pine tree one morning when the sky was filled with ash and smoke, and it began to make us feel uneasy, an old friend perhaps turned dangerous.

And maybe not. Maybe fire will never reach these hills, although the commonly held theory is *not if but when,* an ominous perspective that's hard to ignore in these times of epic droughts and storms and conflagrations.

And maybe the tree would have never snapped or fallen, staying strong and stable, continuing to grow long after we were gone.

This was not a decision made lightly. We called in an expert, Dale Powers. "It's a healthy tree," he concluded. "But there are good reasons to remove it."

This seems to be a season for removing things. Dale returned this morning with his tree-cutting equipment and set about doing so. I watched him as he began his work.

"Do you feel the emotional component of this?" I asked him, because I had suddenly realized I very much did.

"Absolutely," was his reply. "It's never easy to take down a tree. Each one is an individual living being. I get it."

To my surprise, I felt tearful.

"Good-bye, old friend," I said to the pine tree. "Thank you for your steadfast presence all these years."

"Yeah. It's never easy," said Dale. I could tell he understood.

23

HIDDEN CAVE

Fernando Librado's so-called "sitting cave" isn't very far from here, but although nearby, it's hidden, a spot chosen carefully by a man who knew these mountains well. A member of the Chumash tribe whose parents were from Santa Cruz Island, Fernando's birth year is debatable, probably 1839, and he was baptized at the mission in Ventura, then raised at Mission La Purisima (although one source says Santa Ynez). Sometimes known as *Kitsepawit* – he may have been given the name Librado in acknowledgement of his ability to read – he spent much of his later life on ranches near Lompoc and Las Cruces working as a sheepherder and handyman, with an occasional expedition to Tranquillon Peak (on what is now Vandenburg Air Force Base) to gather medicinal plants endemic to its slopes.

My archeologist friend Larry Spanne had memories of Fernando's cave. "My dad took me out there," he said. "It looked like Fernando had put floor boards there, and there were some cans and things lying around the surface. The guy that told my dad and me about it was John Begg, and John Begg knew Fernando personally, and I interviewed him. He told me Fernando was the ranch midwife, medicine man, and doctor. He treated people on the ranch, sheared sheep, and did a lot of things. But he actually lived in that cave."

Although he represented the third generation of Chumash after the initial European colonization of California and therefore had no first-hand knowledge of Chumash life before European contact, Fernando listened attentively to the teachings of his elders and retained a wealth of stories and knowledge in his head. When ethnographer-linguist John P. Harrington encountered him – right here in Gaviota – he became a crucial source of information about Chumash culture and traditions that might otherwise have been lost to time, passing along precious knowledge of the language, religious beliefs, ceremonies, legends, plants, and crafts. In 1912 he famously directed the building of what he called a "house of the sea", i.e., a functional *tomol* based upon the traditional plank canoe construction he recalled from his childhood. I have seen a picture of him taken that year. He is sitting on a wooden chair in Lompoc someplace, white-bearded, wearing shoes, and looking proud, with two young men standing behind him, each with a hand on one of his shoulders, as though tagging time before it gets away. Fernando would have been in his seventies when he died in 1915, but there are stories that claim he lived well beyond his hundredth year – and in a way, he certainly did.

Whether the sitting cave was Fernando's home away from home – or home, period – I jumped at the chance to see it for myself. I was with a historian, two archaeologists, and retired local teacher Bruce Brownell. The idea was to take a look-around for the purposes of official documentation and protection, but it was Mr. Brownell who knew exactly where to find it. (He always considered the backcountry to be an extension of the classroom, so of course he took fourth graders to the sitting cave now and then – who wouldn't?) Our little group gathered in the morning and headed into the mountains.

It is a cave that requires you to bend down a bit for entry, but once within you can stand upright. It would have been a comfortable abode, sheltered and well positioned, with long wide views. Decaying pieces of wood lay on the ground outside the entrance, and when we brushed away some dried brown leaves and dirt, we could see a board with an old iron door hinge attached. One of the archaeologists, a burly fellow, was carrying a stack of typewritten notes and a camera with a big zoom lens. He examined the walls of the cave intently and located a pair of carved initials, allegedly Fernando's, but I can't say they were clear. He took photographs of the carving from every angle, and we all leaned in, looking closely, cramming into a smallish space and being very serious. I could have sworn I heard Fernando chuckling.

But I like knowing there is a sheltered place concealed by brush not far from here where a man once sat who understood the value of story and of passing along what is learned.

"Listen with your heart," I think he whispered. "Write some of it down."

Then again, he might have been pulling my leg.

24

THIS PARTICULAR CREEK

Five million years ago, tectonic forces pushed and lifted the marine rocks of the Santa Barbara coast out of the ocean, creating the Santa Ynez Mountains. Those mountains were carved by erosion, and the fresh water running off their southern flank cut a series of canyons, each with a creek flowing southwest to the sea. Anyway, this is what I have read, and this is how I understand the birth of my creek. It's called Sacate, as is the canyon through which it runs, a name that derives from the Spanish word, *zacate*, for grass, and indeed its hillsides are grassy ones. Cattle have grazed here since at least as far back as the 1790s, when the land was leased by Captain José Francisco Ortega, chief scout of the Portola expedition that ventured into this region in 1769.

As creeks go, I suppose Sacate is an average one, but not to me. I have never before lived by a creek or gotten to know one well, so you can understand my special fondness. It meanders for about two and a half miles, shallow or deep by season, here and there hidden underground, but always running. When my daughter was a little girl, she and Monte walked through it once in tall rubber boots, from near our house all the way down to the main road and the beach, and they said it was like a path through an enchanted land, lush and leafy on either side. After heavy rains, it is turbulent and noisy, rushing through with startling force, rendering portions of the road impassable. One winter, I tromped around in it after a storm and was surprised to find a volleyball among other sundry items that had somehow ended up there.

But it is a welcoming habitat. I have seen shy turtles sunning themselves on its stones, slipping into the water as soon as they sense my presence, and a few days ago, in a place where the water pools like an estuary, I caught a glimpse of a heron stopping by, and a pair of red dragonflies darting about.

Years ago, I slung a woven string hammock from a great sycamore tree by its banks, and it is a sad commentary on my life and personality that I so seldom leaned back and loitered there looking up into the leaves and sky above, listening to creek sounds, but it was lovely when I did, always cool and shady and smelling wonderfully of bark and mulch and creek-water. Rather than wading through it or sitting by it, I mostly walk alongside this creek. If I am going up the canyon, I pass a certain oak whose girth attests to a most respectable age, then a gathering of cottonwoods whose leaves turn truly yellow in the fall, then a stretch of hummingbird sage thriving in the damp mulchy soil, and poison oak in abundance.

Beyond the neighbors' house I can smell the treated wood of a fancy bridge, a grander-than-was-needed act of construction by some investor from Los Angeles, followed shortly by the unmistakable pungency of naturally occurring sulfur, so distinct that I could tell you even blindfolded exactly where I am along the way. Then, near the sandstone formations by the road, the creek diverts and widens, soon births a tributary that wanders toward Cuarta, but continues on its course, more or less.

I have been told that Sacate was one of the more widely traveled roads through here in the old days, leading as it does up and over and ultimately down onto Highway 1, with that faithful and useful creek alongside for such a good portion of the route. There used to be a cross carved into one of the oldest oak trees by the creek, supposedly from the time of the missions and Spanish ranchers. I saw it myself, and I think it was carved more recently than that, but in any case, the tree was lost to wind and weather, one of many older oaks in this section that have fallen recently, retroactive victims of a fire that scorched the area in the 1950s. Although their growth continued bravely, the exposed inner trunks reveal the charred core of a shared history.

But whether or not some cross-carving padre ventured through here, he would have been long preceded by the native people who knew this creek and canyon well. Of this I have no doubt. How compelling would have been a watershed so pleasant and reliable? I imagine the creek silver with steelhead, and processions of quail parading freely, as they still do, and anyone agile could climb up the rocks and hillsides for long views to the sea and Santa Rosa Island. I am certain this little creek was a backdrop to their lives, just as it is to mine. Maybe they heard the comforting din of its roar in the winter, and on spring nights perhaps a splashing of turtles, and the singing of frogs.

Turning around and heading back down the canyon, I see Sacate Creek become a deep gorge by the well, more level with the road as it goes past the house and the orchard, and then etching its own little ravine, finally emptying itself by the ramp at Big Drakes. When it is storm-fed, it has been known to mingle with the sea, a brackish pool of driftwood, kelp, and debris, washing away the access to the beach.

But it's summer now, and my creek is in its shy mode, which doesn't mean it has nothing more to say.

25

JACKSON AND THE GOSPEL CHOIR

It was a rainy February day in a still-new millennium, and the Dunn Middle School students who had enrolled in our oral history and philanthropy electives were arriving at my house in vans to interview Jackson Browne. As far as the kids were concerned, he was not so much an icon as some old musician their parents seemed to like, and they were completely nonchalant. I, on the other hand, had regressed into goofiness, obsessively testing my tape recorder, fluffing sofa pillows, and scribbling back-up questions to have on hand in case the conversation stalled. I even tripped while running up the stairs to grab my camera, landing hard on my rear – an event that was mercifully not witnessed.

I need not have been so nervous. Jackson was gracious, humble, and funny. Justly famous on a global scale as a songwriter, musician, and human rights activist, here at the Ranch he tends to be relaxed, informal, and right at home – because indeed he is at home, having bought property here in 1978. "Even when I was younger," he told us, "I thought it would be great to go out and buy land and not do anything with it, because so much of the land is being developed.

I thought 'I'm gonna buy some land that no one will ever do anything with,' and I found that people were basically doing that here – restricting its uses so it would stay in its natural state. More than just being neighbors, the people up here at the Ranch share a similar philosophy."

Through the window behind him, the light was silvery, and the hills were green, and there was the sound of rain in gentle percussion. "Maybe the most renewing thing is to be by myself at the Ranch," Jackson mused, "and to spend a few days up here just thinking. A friend of mine had a phrase for it. She said, 'That's called leaning up against the cheek of God.' I was trying to explain to her that when you come to my house – I keep saying how beautiful it is, but I'm not telling you about a fabulous house. I'm telling you the house is beautiful because of where it is. The natural beauty…"

Leaning against the cheek of God. I hadn't thought of it that way, but it did seem fitting for the way the sky held us, the tenderness of being here, the sense of nearness to what matters.

Someone asked Jackson if he was religious. "I'm not a member of an organized religion or faith, but the truth is, I am religious. I think I practice a kind of religion, though I don't have to say that I do at all. A friend of mine is director of the gospel choir at a high school in Los Angeles. He lets me come, and I love this music – these kids are so amazing – as a matter of fact, if you could ever get Fred Martin and his kids to come to your school, any way to make it happen, I would try to help. This music is a tremendous force in their lives; it comes from the Baptist tradition, a certain ethnic place in our culture. They're definitely singing the praises of God…"

What if… yes, I was already snagged on the idea of Fred Martin and the gospel choir, that brief aside about figuring out a way to bring them to our community. I glanced over at my colleagues Linda

Smith and Lynne Castellanos and saw the same spark in their eyes. I knew this would be our next project.

"The closest thing I belong to that's like a church," Jackson was saying, "is a group of friends that over the course of twenty or thirty years have probably done hundreds and hundreds of benefit performances to raise funds for a variety of causes. There's no name for us. We call ourselves 'the usual suspects' or funny names like 'the bleeding hearts' – we know about each other because we're always asking each other to do things."

I hoped that the kids were picking up on all this: a circle of friends who do things for others, the activist approach, the idea of being constructively and compassionately alive in the world. And while Jackson's life is admittedly extraordinary, he warned us not to underrate our own: "When you think about it, probably more than half of what's on television is selling you some notion that there are some beautiful people someplace, and you can find out about them, and you can be like them if you tune in, and buy stuff that they buy, or go where they go… That's all crap. That's complete and utter crap. That's to say that their lives are more valuable than yours."

Jackson urged the students to develop a sense of what is right and wrong and real, and never to underestimate what they might accomplish. "As much as I love the world," he said, "there are fights out there. There are some fights that are coming your way. Don't back down from what you know is right. And in the end, you are the one to decide."

We talked for two hours. Now the light had dimmed, the rain continued, and it suddenly felt late. It was time to get the kids in the vans and back to campus. They descended the steps laughing and chatting and colorful as confetti, all that wonderful middle school energy – and I wonder, nearly twenty years later, how much they remember of their afternoon with Jackson Browne, whether they hear his songs differently, or if they have incorporated any of his advice into their thinking long term. You never know what sticks.

But there was still the matter of the gospel choir. And it wasn't easy, but a concert was arranged, and one morning the following May, a bus set out from South Central Los Angeles to the Santa Ynez Valley with Fred Martin, the Washington Preparatory High School gospel singers, and an assortment of instruments and equipment on board. St. Mark's Episcopal Church in Los Olivos, with Father Stacey at the helm, had agreed to be the venue for an evening performance, but first there came an impromptu noon concert on the Dunn School campus, which no one who was there will ever forget. Fred, who is himself a remarkable young musician and teacher, charmed everyone, and the voices of the singers, among whom I particularly remember Chavonne Morris and Alethea Mills, were somehow both angelic and electrifying. They performed a bit of R & B and Motown, but mostly it was good old-fashioned gospel, and the spirit infused us all. Everyone – students, teachers, staff, even the younger children who had come by from the nearby Family School – were clapping and dancing and singing along, making a joyful noise.

The magic resumed at the church later, and the house of God was a full one that night, and it seemed to me the building may have lifted off the ground. Friendships began, and all of us were giddy, and in my heart, I felt a sense that really anything was possible. I don't recall if there was a moon that night, but I know that there was light, and we were shimmering like angels.

Jackson Browne was smiling in the back of the church. Afterwards I figure he went back to the Ranch and leaned up against the cheek of God.

26

A SHIP PILED HIGH WITH ORANGES

My friend Mr. Harbor called me from England one November morning. Perhaps it was his tea time and he had an urge to chat. Sometimes he gets a bit downhearted, you see. He told me that a special book was in the post on its way to me, a beautiful book about Cornwall that his daughter gave to him in 1976, and now he has inscribed it for me, and he thinks I will enjoy the style of writing and the place it is about, but it will also represent a link between our families.

It's no small thing when someone takes a long-cherished book signed by a daughter and sends it on to you, and I shall receive it humbly and with full appreciation of its significance. Then we talked about daughters a bit, for each of us has one, and a quote by J.M. Barrie came to mind: *Fame is rot; daughters are the thing.* It is a thought that always makes me sigh with agreement, although lately I inevitably feel a little shortchanged too, because mine is both singular and absent, becoming an abstraction, capable of happiness but having chosen a kind found only faraway.

"There's an early frost on the ground here," Mr. Harbor tells me, and for a moment I picture the daughter that is mine in her perennial flip-flops, toes getting numb, but she has probably switched to boots by now.

Mr. Harbor, whom she indirectly brought into my life by virtue of his being the grandfather of her husband-to-be, is quite tender and sympathetic on the subject of daughters getting cold, but he believes that the kids have plenty of duvets, even if their house is drafty. His worries are more substantial, extending far beyond this winter and trudging deep into a future where he fears those young people will face hard times and bleak prospects. I respond with my usual talk of hope and better outcomes; I'm good for that. But Mr. Harbor remains unconvinced, for he is, he says, a pessimist and a cynic.

You know what bothers him especially? That those *scoundrels* always get away with it. They'll go on to live richly while others are struggling. Such terrible inequities. So little justice, really. But that's always been the way of the world, hasn't it? A man could get bitter, watching it all unfold.

But there are other thoughts to travel along. There is something Mr. Harbor still dreams about that happened long ago. It's not for me to tell you here, but it's funny how fresh those old hurts and desires can seem, how stunning and real even way past the time in which they mattered.

The world was different when Mr. Harbor was young, but it comes in clear sometimes, the things you wanted and almost had. And what you actually had and somehow lost, maybe that's the most painful one of all.

"Even as a child, I was always a bit quirky," Mr. Harbor tells me now. "Once I wrote the time on a piece of paper, rolled it up, and placed it in the archway of a long row of terraced houses."

"Like a time capsule?" I asked.

"Yes. My cousin found it and wondered what it meant. Another time, while waiting to catch the train, I was seized with emotion and wrote my name on the signal box. It was there for ages. No one ever knew whose name it was or why it was there."

It's an understandable impulse, the yearning to be remembered, to leave some evidence of having passed through.

Mr. Harbor's formative years were shaped by events that I cannot fully imagine. His mother died when he was in his teens, and then of course there was the war, looming everywhere, ending any chances for a carefree youth. "I was eighteen, and quickly absorbed into war work," he told me once. "I worked twelve hours a day. I was uneducated, but they saw in me the potential to learn a skill and a lasting trade in machinery engineering. I had a blessed calling."

He had a blessed marriage, too. It has been a few years since his wife died, and he misses her every day. This is a hard part of life. He is unmoored – *melancholy*, to use another of his words. And he worries a lot, but this isn't new. "You're either a worrier or not," says Mr. Harbor. "I was born worrying."

You know, it isn't easy being here with your mind so crisp and your life so narrowed down, when your own pen won't write with the clarity in your head, and ruminations turn to gloom.

It is better to stay tangible, and here in the present. Set the table, be seated, comport yourself with dignity. Let your mind rest on concrete thoughts: bridges, books, and bicycles, Mousehole Harbour crowded with boats.

Consider oranges, perhaps.

"Ah, yes, how is the weather in California?" Mr. Harbor asks.

I tell him, mild, warm, autumnal slant of light.

"I wish," says Mr. Harbor, "that you could go outside and pick me some oranges and somehow I would have them here on my table in twenty-four hours."

Oh, I'll pick you oranges, I tell him, as soon as the crop really comes in. Yes, I'll pick you oranges and ship them to you! (Perhaps I can really do this, I think... for I am thrilled to have a mission.)

And I understand all at once that Mr. Harbor is not as pessimistic or cynical as he claims to be, nor is he bitter. He is disappointed, perhaps, and troubled on behalf of those he loves, but Mr. Harbor remains sentimental at the core of him, with a residue of romance.

Who among us doesn't sometimes feel a bit sad at the first sign of frost and the dimming light of early evening?

"Ah," says Mr. Harbor, "a *ship*. I am picturing a ship piled high with oranges sailing across the sea to me. That is a picture I shall keep."

The last time I saw Mr. Harbor, he was ninety-six years old and had moved into a care home near Oxford. His daughter visited him frequently, but I decided that while I was in the area, I should come by too. I admit I had trepidations. There is something depressing about these facilities: the vaguely institutional smells, the muffled, mustered-up cheeriness, the frail and baffled residents. Indeed, although this place was excellent, its ambiance immediately evoked memories of my mother's long stay in the one in California, which churned me up a bit. But I also remembered how happy she was when a friendly visitor appeared at her door. It was a special occasion to her, a bright moment in her dreary stretch of limbo days.

So we opened the big double entry doors, walked down a corridor, and entered Mr. Harbor's room.

I had not expected him to look so small and fragile in his bed. He was pale and hollow-cheeked, his glasses were on the bedside table, and his voice when he spoke was barely audible. His daughter whispered to me that he was sleepy and not as lucid as he had been the day before.

"Look who has come to see you," she told him. "All the way from California. Remember Cynthia?"

"Ah, yes," he said. "I do indeed."

And as I leaned in closer to him, he took my hand and kissed it.

27

TEXT MESSAGE

I want to write about here and now because the macadamia trees are in bloom, dangles of pink, intoxicatingly fragrant, and there is a chorus of bees in the orchard. Pollinators. Life affirmers. The place is humming in surround-sound, and it feels like the song of the universe. I step onto a narrow path and walk among the trees: bracelets of blossoms, heady scent, sunlight and shadow.

Monarch butterflies too, presumably on their way to Mexico, have discovered that this is a very pleasant space in which to linger. I see them flitting about, alighting on the flowers, opening their wings, pausing for a nectar sip, and taking off again, like golden wishes aflutter in a blue sky. It's a day that is glaringly bright, and it dazzles me, seeming surreal, or even psychedelic.

I am wholly alive in a holy place. The orchard becomes my cathedral, leaves and blooms and branches filtering the sunlight like stained glass, and the thrumming buzz of the bees is the choir of the cosmos, or perhaps its heartbeat, as much a pulse as a sound.

I wander to the citrus grove by the fence and gather a few ripe grapefruit that had been dislodged from the trees by yesterday's wind.

They are comically large, and my bag is soon heavy, and I'll squeeze them later for their tart, refreshing juice.

As I approach the house, I hear the ding of a text message, and it's my friend Barbara saying hello from Manhattan, where, she says, it is "global-warmingly hot" and she's going to see Michael Moore's show, craving some hope and humor in lieu of her daily cry, and I know exactly what she means.

But I'm also struck by how incongruous and amazing it is that I am standing on the dirt in Gaviota with a sack of grapefruit in my hands, having real-time contact with someone about to enter a theater on Broadway, and I'm buoyed a bit by the knowledge that we are going through this moment in history together, and that wonders do abound, and there is so much hope and possibility in the spacious and gracious implausibility of it all.

28

GIRL WITH A SUITCASE

I'm fond of those little Ranch girls, watched from a distance as they pretend, conspire, and tell each other secrets. They come as they are, or however they feel like being. An outfit built around a frilly mesh skirt with pink tights serves just as well as a hand-me-down tee shirt from a brother or dungarees and cowboy boots. Tiaras and wands are optional.

They can be a bit exclusive. They have their own things going on and no need for some old lady, benign as she might be, to ask them silly questions or document their antics. But I do know this. The one whose name is Milly, when asked what she wanted for Christmas, said: a suitcase. I keep thinking that's like a little poem in itself.

There was also poetry in the bobcat who strolled up our driveway on Christmas Eve, in no hurry at all, then detoured into the orchard and was last seen scampering under the fence along the creek. Those oranges were like poems, heaped in a blue bowl, and that crazy moon above the hills last night proliferating shadows and lozenges of light. There was a visit with ninety-five-year-old Mr. Harbor in England, blinking through a computer screen. There was Monte standing at the shore, reading the waves, paddling out.

My father-in-law at ninety sat in his La-Z-Boy playing rousing music on his iPad, a newfangled device he has grown fond of. It's vintage Czechoslovakian polka music, he says, and it makes him happy, so it becomes the soundtrack for the morning. My mother-in-law was reading an old dog-eared book on native plants, making plans, enjoying her own notes from years past written in the margins. Their window looks out onto a creek bed and the canyon road beyond. The cottonwood trees are in their brief season of yellow leaves, and a toyon by the house is a bounty of red berries, and wisps of cloud are rolling above the newly green hills. My daughter was visiting, and there she was, removing her muddy wellies outside the door, having just returned from the well… and one was tempted to say all is well.

Oh, I certainly know all is not well. I happened to run into Yvon Chouinard recently. I thanked him for what his company, Patagonia, did on the day after Thanksgiving, donating 100 per cent of their sales to help the environment. His modest response: "It's only money." And I said, "Yeah. We're all going to hell in a hand-basket anyway." And he said, "That's right." He always seems kind of Buddhist about things, or maybe fatalistic. Might as well go down doing something.

Meanwhile, I've been having an ongoing dialog with my friend Dave about anger. I admit to anger; Dave either doesn't feel it or refuses to acknowledge it. His Holiness the Dalai Lama would disapprove, he tells me – anger is just poison, diminishing our credibility and causing only harm. Dave's dismissal of my anger makes me angry, of course. I realize we cannot get swept up into useless drama with each new outrage, but anger is an understandable human response to the daily assaults on our values and the exasperating mentality that brought us to this point. I see it as an alarm, a clarifying energy born of conscience. The trick is to figure out how to channel it constructively.

One day I went into the sweet little town of Los Olivos and stopped by to see my friend Dorothy on Figueroa Mountain Road. We talked about what strengths and resources we have, what strategies we can employ, how to sustain our energy through the long run, using our anger as a fuel but humor too, and love, mostly love. We looked out at the mountains. The world is so beautiful, she said.

California Christmas. A Mexican woman was selling homemade tamales wrapped like presents in foil and brown paper, still warm. A neighbor gave us a bowl of sweet persimmons, the kind you eat like apples. I rode my bicycle when the sandstone cliffs were golden and the green hills luminous, feeling exhilarated and inexplicably strong. There have been low-low tides and a sea as calm and quiet as I have ever seen it. My daughter was curled up on the living room sofa in a shaft of sunlight, reading, and I saw three former students in the course of a week, all good people, all grown up. Such encounters make me feel I mattered a little.

I heard a wonderful podcast interview (Krista Tippett's *On Being*) with poet Paul Muldoon recently, and he talked about poetry as a process of revelation. And when Krista asked him what he had learned about life (a question I am fond of asking when I interview people, but which often tends to silence them) his answer was basically, "The thing I know now, and I'm sure this is true of many, is how – not even how little I know, but how I know nothing, in fact."

I happen to be exactly the same age as Paul Muldoon, and I have lately been feeling just that way. He talked a bit further about all the mysteries and questions, the potential existence of universes plural, in

GIRL WITH A SUITCASE

fact billions of them, and concluded: "To try to take that in is almost impossible, yet, I suppose, we must try, on this tiny planet … to do our best while we're here. And I think, really, our impulse is to do our best, however often we might lose sight of it, and we can try to be kind-ish to one another while we're still here."

I like that. Be kind-ish to one another while we're still here. And also, be open to the poetry, the shifts in thinking, the new ways of looking that unearth revelations. Like those little girls in the field by the sea, whispering secrets, one of them wishing for a suitcase. I wonder what she will pack. I wonder what journeys she will take.

29

THE WEIGHT OF THINGS

My friends Ming and David came out on Sunday for our annual New Year's walk, only six months late. After coffee and croissants, we headed for the beach. The air was warm and humid, the shore was heaped with tangles of kelp, and little flies hovered about our faces. We detoured first to see the state of the whale that had died at sea in January and washed up onto the sand. It lies there now in graphic decomposition, having gradually become part of the landscape, from a distance just a mound of darkened sand, and in close-up a crash course in mortality.

What does it say about us that we visit it like a shrine, or point it out to friends as though it were a local landmark? We respect the majesty of its being, are shocked at the enormity of its death, and at the same time are morbidly fascinated by its remains – that something this large, once living, is becoming earth and dust before our eyes. The crowd of vultures, gulls and occasional coyotes that initially came to peck and feast on the carcass have long since abandoned it to ruin. Its discolored skin has collapsed like a tent, here and there is the shock of bone exposed, and a vacated eye socket stares blankly into eternity.

We each bring something of ourselves to it. David, a veterinarian, points out a few anatomical features, although they are present only like Dali's melting pocket watches, gone soft and shapeless, devoid of purpose, for time takes all, and even time is taken. Ming leans down to look more closely, falls silent, and gradually slides into a kneel, honoring the spirit once housed within this vessel. She gently touches what we think is skull and closes her eyes for a moment. She holds a quiver of raggedy feathers and a broken bit of abalone shell, treasures gathered as we walked. Ming is young, and open to the everything-ness, even when it overwhelms. And I am the one who suggests we get going.

Elsewhere, there are families on the beach, umbrellas and coolers, children and dogs, a kind of playful chaos that I remember well.

Doing things I used to do
They think are new

Yes, I know it's maudlin and melancholy, but that phrase from an old song I remember being sung by Marianne Faithfull is what comes into my head. Who can explain how fast it all goes by? Then there comes a time of reinvention. That's where I'm at now. I walk on the beach with shoes and jeans, a part of the scene but apart from it, zig-zagging and wobbly. I'm trying to learn.

And that reminds me: there is a cattle scale at the corral at San Augustine that I've been curious about, the oldest in Santa Barbara County, and it isn't far to walk from here, and wouldn't it be cool to have our veterinarian friend explain how it works?

We walk a little further west, inland, uphill, and across a railroad track to an area where fencing, cattle chutes, and other old structures from the ranching operations are clustered. The wood housing that encloses the scale has recently been rebuilt, but the scale itself has been in use since 1892, is still used today, and is known for its accuracy. Based on the design and time frame, David speculates that it is a Fairbanks scale, and he tells me about the Fairbanks brothers of Vermont, Erastus and Thaddeus, who developed an accurate and stable weighing machine in the 1820s. The Fairbanks scale used an arrangement of four supporting levers lowered into a pit, and a platform level with the ground, ending the task of having to hoist the entire load. It was patented in 1830 and by 1882 the company was producing 80,000 scales annually, both standard and custom.

David's an enthusiastic teacher. He points out the route the cattle would take to get onto the platform, and he shows us the balances and counter-balances, and he talks about feed conversion, weight loss, and profitability. There's a whole science to this, and accuracy is crucial. A red and white seal shows that our scale has been certified by the Santa Barbara County Department of Agriculture Weights and Measures, which is very exciting, but I find my attention drawn to the beautiful rippled patterns and complex texture of the weathered wood fencing, the comforting chug and whistle of a passing freight train, the familiar golden hills framed in the window of a barn.

Meanwhile Ming has discovered a tiny, emaciated calf with a patch over its eye in a nearby corral. On first glance, David doesn't think the prognosis is great, but maybe, with the special care it is evidently getting, the poignant little animal might manage to pull through. Just another small drama quietly unfolding...

We talk and fall silent in comfortable waves, and we inevitably get to the heart of things. Still in the ascending arch of her early thirties, Ming has life events to share, the kind that seem to come at you fast, ground shifting when you've barely found your footing. And it's all a

119

great adventure but there is also a fire nearby and the threat of evacuation, and a relationship that hasn't really launched, and the college debt that feels impossible to climb out of, and most of all, there is the disillusionment of what is happening since the 2016 election.

"I grew up in a hopeful time," she tells us. She didn't know that misogyny and racism were still so prevalent, that our democracy could be under siege as it is, and everything we care about threatened. "I guess I don't feel hopeful anymore," she says.

I know what she means. The weight of the world is bearing down on us all. But I was an idealistic new teacher once, one of hope's intrepid foot soldiers, and Ming, in fact, was in my class back then, more than twenty years ago. And I still believe that my role is to act in hopeful ways, particularly as an elder. It's dangerous to flirt with despair, or even give it leeway as an option. When it comes to despair, I'm deliberately in denial. I think despair, like hope, is a self-fulfilling prophecy.

Oh, I admit that life was easier when I didn't understand how fleeting it is, when I didn't know that rather than abating, loss compounds, and time heals nothing. Life was easier when I wasn't bombarded moment by moment by news near and far, when I thought that suffering was not in vain and some kind of everything-will-be-okay-ness ultimately awaited.

Now it all weighs so heavy, it's hard to stand up. But I point out legitimate victories to my young friend and remind her that unanticipated developments are yet to come, some of which will be wonderful. We cannot be the ones who gave up.

When we three get together, we have a little ritual before we say good-bye. Ming calls it "postcards to the universe". Some might call it prayer. We speak what is in our hearts, what we would want in the year ahead. On this occasion, David begins. "Dear Universe," he says.

"This is not so much a postcard or a request, but rather a statement of intent. I hereby resolve not to try so hard to control everything. I intend to have a lighter touch, to trust the give and take, the natural ebbs and flows, to navigate gently and know that we cannot force things."

Ming's postcard is essentially a wish and a summoning of strength, and mine is mostly gratitude for love and wonder, and an oft-stated hope that we'll get through this dark time, as a nation and in our own lives, maybe even emerging better than we were, more cognizant, more engaged. Maybe something like faith will reassert itself without all this exhaustive effort to pretend it isn't shaken. My heart is heavy, but there's still a spark within. And sparks upon sparks can light the world.

30

SHOOTING STARS

It's just the way I am. If there's going to be a meteor shower, I want to watch. And so last night I hauled a sleeping bag, pad, and pillow out onto the deck. My original plan had been to set a clock for 3:30 a.m. and go out between moonset and dawn when the sky would be darkest and the meteors brightest, but since I couldn't sleep anyway, I decided around midnight to assume my post.

I tend to think of the nights here as silent except for the occasional high-pitched coyote song and frogs in their season, but as soon as I settled myself outdoors I remembered that the air contains a constant undercurrent of sound. It enveloped me like a rich and complex tapestry: clicks and hums, murmurings of an of owl, animal scratchings in the brush nearby, and whisperings of wind in a tree whose black shadowy shape became as familiar to me as a friend. There's so much happening constantly that eludes our notice. I lay there as my eyes adjusted to the dark. The moon, a quarter full, cast its pale light like a filtering lens, and swaths of the sky were white with the Milky Way, but as I watched, the darkness deepened, and there were stars of startling brightness everywhere. I scanned the sky, trying too

123

hard, impatient for a reward, and then with my peripheral vision saw a thin line of light zoom by, and minutes later... whoa!... a blazingly bright, thick streak, shooting by too fast for a double take but memorable indeed. Now *that* was a shooting star.

Long waits in between. Watching a meteor shower takes a good deal of patience. I'd read that this year's Perseid shower would be an "outburst" and might yield as many as 200 meteors in an hour, so it seemed to me that one or two a minute was a reasonable expectation, but expectation is not an appropriate state of mind in these situations. I tried to get comfortable and simply key in to the pleasure of being present to witness this jeweled summer night, just me and the same vast sky my ancestors once beheld.

On the other hand, never mind about my ancestors. I'm pretty sure they would have been far too exhausted and weary from their daily labors to indulge in luxurious bouts of pre-planned sky-watching, intent on seeing a particular quota of meteors. No, for them it would have been a matter of happenstance, of looking up in the very astonishing moment a meteor was shooting through the heavens, and the more romantic among them would have seen it as a gift or an omen, and possibly made a wish. And oh, their wishes have rolled down through the ages and found their way into my heart. I was born with yearning in my DNA.

As were we all, perhaps, for it is the state of being human... is it not? To be alive involves a continual wanting and reaching, a struggle to stay upright despite crushing sorrow and the awareness of our own brevity, an ancient kind of yearning that only ceases in brief moments of one-ness and forgetting, or with the elusive equanimity that comes with enlightenment.

And there I was, lying on a sleeping bag with the very cosmos shining before my eyes, thinking in those tiresome human terms.

Another flamboyant meteor shot by above the hills to the east, a beauty with a long wide trail of light. And another, just beyond my field of vision, was as pale and small as a white moth in the distance, but moving straight and fast, a jet-propelled glide into its vanishing. I began to rest in the spaces between. I felt that old familiar mix of insignificance and wonder, humbled to have been given the privilege of bearing witness, of being somehow part of it all, fleetingly and forever. I let go of the personal history and opened myself up to whatever unknown vastness and mystery encompassed me. In short, I fell asleep.

I awoke just in time for what was supposed to have been the peak of the peak, the hour for which I had initially planned to get of bed and begin my vigil. But coastal clouds had moved in as I slept, and the sky was blank, not a star in sight. I gathered my things, slipped into the house, and went back to bed, satisfied.

PART IV

BEARING WITNESS

O my love,
O it was a funny little thing
to be the ones to've seen.
   – Joanna Newsom

31

HARBOR OF GRACE

Peering at the rain-smeared night through the windows of the air-port bus makes me feel the way I used to feel in the 1970s when I was a girl in my twenties sitting on Greyhound buses, lost and con-fused, maybe a fledgling feminist but not familiar with the term, a passenger in my own life. Perhaps I should give myself credit for the courage that I had, but I certainly wasted a lot of time in sad pursuits and misguided getaways. This time, I'm on a mission, heading for the Women's March in Washington, with a rather indirect itinerary: Los Angeles to Charlotte to Albany. From Albany, I'll drive with my old friend Barbara to Maryland, where friends of hers will host us.

When I first arrive, the weather in Albany is what I recall as vintage upstate New York: a muted palette of gray, brown, and white. Chilly. I go out for a walk after arriving at Barb's house, careful about the icy driveway, the walkways patched with snow and frozen slush. My hands are cold; I hadn't thought of wearing gloves. A woman pulls up in a car in front of a house nearby and steps outside to check her mailbox. She smiles. "Enjoying the nice, mild weather?" It's all rela-tive, I suppose.

Meanwhile, back home, the rain has finally stopped and there are rainbows arched above green hills. Monte texts me: *Sacate Creek is flowing!* The campground at El Capitan has washed away in mud. The ocean is the color of chocolate milk and waterfalls have surprised old sandstone contours. The world is many worlds, constantly changing, and reality itself seems fluid and unbound.

But there *is* a structure of truth and principle, and there *are* foundations we build upon and cherish, and that's why I'm marching on Saturday. I'm marching because I care about human rights, and fairness, and dignity, and possibility, and the fate of our poor beleaguered planet. I'm marching because the person about to assume office, who in fact lost the popular vote by millions, is dangerously unfit to serve. I want him to see that he does not have our support, and I want to help promote and partake of the solidarity and determination that I know we're going to need to sustain us through the hard times ahead.

"A march? It's as pointless as a temper tantrum," I heard someone say mockingly. But I believe, as Rebecca Solnit has written, that symbolic and cultural acts have real power. I am hoping the march will energize us, render visible our national and global community, reinforce the sense of possibility, speak our truths, tell our stories, and mark a beginning rather than a descent into defeat and resignation. We march to push back against the affronts being perpetrated upon us and to help launch the resistance. I realize it's just the start, and long hard work must follow, but a start is required.

The next day, we set out for D.C. in Barbara's car: Barb (at the wheel), her friend (and soon my friend too) Ronda, and me. There's a percussion of raindrops and windshield wipers, the murmur of conversation, a soundtrack of songs from *Hamilton*, a smattering of Joni Mitchell, and good old Jackson Browne.

130

Barb and I became friends in the 1970s, not long after my desperado Greyhound bus days. I was belatedly wrapping up a degree at the state university, and she was a newly minted social worker, and we happened to both live in an old brownstone building at the edge of downtown Albany. We would visit each other at the end of the day, debriefing, listening to records (often Jackson Browne), and coaching one another through what I still refer to as the days of whine and roaches. (You could actually hear those roaches in the night, a sort of tapping-crunching sound, and if you turned on a light, you could see them scurrying across the floor.) We found the humor too, and we became dear to one another, but life took us in different directions, and forty years happened with no contact between us. We reconnected only recently, and we instantly clicked. It was as though she had just walked back in from across the hallway with a new album for us to hear.

Thank God for friendship, especially among women. I don't know how I would navigate life without such friends. And oh, how women talk! Our car becomes a sanctuary of stories and warmth and camaraderie, a harbor of grace, it seems. Ronda sets out a bag of nuts, a container of celery sticks and carrots, green grapes, Cliff bars. We tend to one another. Even in this transition zone, a demonstration has begun, and it sets the tone for what we are about to witness: mutual support, kindness, and resilience.

The "inauguration" is taking place as we drive, and we don't know if we can bear to listen. Ronda, an insightful psychologist who is exceptionally devoted to her clients and her own three sons, counsels against denial. "If we don't listen at all, that's just intentional ignorance," she says, and we decide to tune in now and then. What we hear sounds militant, ominous, chilling... a dark vision of carnage and fear, a false and eerie patriotism, a rally to total allegiance.

131

Ronda's mother, now in her nineties, is a Holocaust survivor who spent two years hidden in a small underground space – *the grave* is what she calls it. The family lived in what is now Ukraine, and as the horrors mounted, Ronda's grandmother sat by the window, planning. One midnight, she bundled up her three children – Ronda's mother, at ten, was the eldest – and walked to the house of a man she vaguely knew who did "illegal things" and asked for his help. They were led to a hole in the dirt beneath a pigsty, with a covering too low to stand up beneath it. It was swarming with vermin and lice. Pig urine rained on their heads.

Ronda's mother has barely spoken of it, except in fragments of poems in old journals, not in English. Decades later, Ronda went back to the Ukraine with her, and they stopped at the house the family had to abandon. A Ukrainian woman came to the door, and with trepidation let them in. Ronda's mother recognized the furniture, the parquet floor, the very window beside which Ronda's grandmother had sat and stared and schemed. The Ukrainian woman cried. She was only a child then. Her parents had taken her to a ditch where they lined up the Jews, shot them, then hastily covered them with dirt. "The ground was heaving," she said. The townspeople watched.

"How did everyone allow this?" asks Ronda. "What happens *matters*. And this is why I'm marching tomorrow."

In Maryland, where the Susquehanna River meets the Chesapeake Bay, we pass a city called Havre de Grace, and the name assumes a serendipitous significance, as do so many aspects of this journey. I admit that I had some anxiety and skepticism when I first contemplated the trip, but my conviction is growing with every mile.

At some point, Barb checks in with her mother, another nonagenarian. "Why are you going to Washington?" her mother says. "I'm looking at the TV, and there's a big commotion there."

"Mom, it's a protest," Barb explains, to no avail. Commotion is worrisome. Distance is daunting. Daughters are precious. A mother worries.

"A march is when bodies speak by walking," writes Rebecca Solnit in *Hope in the Dark*, "[It's] when private citizens become that mystery the public, when traversing boulevards of cities becomes a way to travel toward political goals."

We will not have stood by in silence.

We arrive in Silver Springs as darkness falls and find our way to the house of our hosts, Jeff and Bonnie, who are easygoing and welcoming and seem immediately familiar to me, even though I have never met them. Maybe it's our Brooklyn roots, shared sensibilities, a similar perspective on what's happening. We reminisce about pizza and knishes, the sawdust on the floors of butcher shops and produce markets, lining up at school to have sugar cubes and a drop of Salk vaccine placed upon our tongues. We discuss the old neighborhoods, the public schools we went to, the work and dreams of our fathers, the things we learned to value.

Ronda's twenty-one-year-old son Jared, a college student in the area, comes by to visit and bring us his firsthand observations of D.C. on this Inauguration Day. It was crazy, he tells us, but not in a celebratory way. Sitting at the table with a group of slightly fraying sixty-somethings, Jared asks if our participation in tomorrow's march feels as significant to us as protests of the past. Absolutely. Unequivocally. Even *more* so. Yes. We all agree on this. The threat is real and profound. The need to resist is crucial, compelling. It's an historical moment.

I think Jared is proud of his mom. In a nod to Joni Mitchell, he calls the three of us women "Ladies of the Canyon," and it seems like an appellation of honor. I picture the California canyon of my home, then feel the comforting old embrace of East Coast-ness, and for a moment, everything comes full circle.

As soon as we board the Metro the next morning, we can feel that something is happening, and we are part of it. There are groups of friends carrying posters, parents with little girls in pink hats, men and women, Boomers and Millennials, and certainly those in between. Everyone is pouring into the city, filling up the trains, and the mood is friendly but not festive. We recognize each other. We're in this together. We have a shared sense of mission and resolve.

We disembark at Union Station, and our numbers keep multiplying... pink hats ascending escalators, patiently lining up for a pre-march restroom stop, streaming out onto the streets. A policeman at the station tells us that the men's room is open to women today. He's good-natured and friendly and admits that this is the happy day. Yesterday? Not so much. More like the twilight zone.

Outside, the air is fresh and the sky a broad white slate of cloud and fog. The pre-march rally has begun, but we are far from it, and we will only see it later in replay at Jeff and Bonnie's house. Right now we just walk in the general direction of the starting point until we abruptly cannot walk, because the street is completely clogged with people. Absolute gridlock. It's the sort of thing that would usually make me claustrophobic, but this is where the miracle begins, because despite the frustration and discomfort, everyone is patient, polite, respectful, and considerate.

At one point, a young woman begins to hyperventilate and needs to get through, and the crowd immediately makes a path for her,

like Moses parting the Red Sea, many looking on with maternal concern as she passes, offering water, asking if she needs anything. Four
Vanderbilt coeds have driven through the night from Nashville to be
there, one of them wheelchair-bound due to a broken foot; strangers
form a barrier around them to give them a little extra space. In the
course of the entire day, there will not be a single episode of violence.

But where is the march? We want to march, and we've come a
long way to do so, and here we are just inching along or standing
still, unable to reach the route! Suddenly we realize: we ARE the
march. The original river has formed a hundred tributaries, the flood-
gates are open, and we are flowing. All of Washington, D.C.
becomes a great, epic march.

Eventually we are marching alongside a small band called Brick
by Brick, a public art performance group that builds human "walls"
against misogyny. They are wearing brick-patterned jumpsuits, carrying signs in protest of actions that threaten civil and human rights,
and making wonderful music. We march along singing "This Land
Is Your Land", "Down by the Riverside", "Swing Low Sweet Char-
iot"... traditional songs of protest, hope and yearning. There's something about the music that really does it to me, along with the sights
of the Washington Monument, the Capitol, the Lincoln Memorial in
the distance, and the messages on the signs that people are carrying,
some of them blunt, some witty, collectively a kind of poetry of the
people, and there is a feeling of extraordinary unity and unshakeable
determination. My eyes fill with tears. My heart fills with hope. Half
a million people? A million? Who knows. We are everywhere. We
are a harbor. We are the sea.

32

ALIGNMENT

It was a last-minute invitation, and I said yes. My friend Linette and her sister Luanne were driving up to Oregon to see the total eclipse. There would be one overnight stop in Gilroy, where Linette's sister-in-law lives, onward to Bend the next morning, and from Bend to a ranch-turned-campground in Mitchell, a small Oregon town (population 130) eighty miles from Bend and directly in the path of totality. There would be five of us in the cab of a Ford truck, and we had all heard the dire warnings about crowds, gas shortages, and traffic in gridlock. Camping would be involved too, an activity that I had long ago filed under the heading of "never again." I looked up the distance between Buellton and Mitchell: 850 miles.

I had already accepted that this glorified total eclipse was not in the cards for me, and I was fine with that, so it's hard to say what compelled me to that yes. All I know is that Linette's enthusiastic invitation was remarkably well timed. I'd been feeling stuck, and I needed to be dislodged, and now a magic carpet had landed at my house. All the planning had been done; I needed only to step on board. So I glossed over the discomforts and challenges of the excursion and focused on the opportunity to glimpse a wondrous celestial event. I wanted to leave myself behind and stand in the shadow of the moon. I wanted to see the shimmer of the solar corona and the color of the sky.

And I said yes, and I joined the eclipse chasers, and now I was in the backseat wedged between two women I had never met before. We traveled northbound along highways and side roads, past rivers and lakes and a national forest, through small towns with diners and convenience stores and vacant motels and streets lined with American flags, with junkyards and gravel pits at their outskirts, and refineries and lumber mills, and barns that said *Jesus Saves*, and a bright purple Victorian house perched on a rise under muffled hazy skies. We stayed in a cabin with rough wood walls, and orange and yellow window coverings that gave everything a 1970s glow, and our host that night recited haiku poetry about hope and alignment, and I remembered when I went to Oregon from New York via Greyhound bus at the age of twenty-four, how little I knew. How little I know.

I bolted awake each morning at the cusp of daylight, feeling chilly and unrested, craving coffee, a dull headache hovering at the edge of my skull. Camping was the part I liked least, and I'll never understand the appeal of sleeping on the ground and stumbling around in the dark, every mundane act transformed into a veritable expedition, but I suppose it's a means to an end, as it was in this case. I'm afraid I wasn't very helpful with things like setting up the tent or lighting the stove, but I became adept at getting out of the way, and I tried to be pleasant and unobtrusive, although I was always looking for something, sorting through my stuff, rustling like a mouse. I'm probably annoying.

The camping area was a thousand-acre cattle ranch dotted by pine trees. We chose a site in a flat open field of blonde grass, with a narrow stream burbling through, and a sparkling reservoir in the distance. There were very few people there when we first arrived, but by Saturday night, campers were closer and more numerous. Three little boys, one named Arlo, were playing by the stream, setting twig boats to sail. A hippie-esque young mother with long yellow hair was overseeing an impromptu lemonade business run by her enterprising daughters. There were scents of pot and propane in the air, and the sounds of laughter and conversation and cattle nearby expressing their noisy bewilderment. Everyone was there for the same reason, and a festive atmosphere prevailed.

We ventured out and explored the Painted Hills and John Day Fossil Beds, hiking amidst weirdly beautiful rock formations in glaring sunlight, and we walked on a path through tall rushes to a river, where everyone but me went in. Most important, we scoped out the site where we would view the eclipse on Monday morning, ascending a hill to a high meadow area with a wide view, where we could observe the whole progression of the shadow crossing.

The long-awaited morning broke still and clear. We dismantled our camp, packed the truck, drove a mile or two along a dirt road, parked, and climbed the hill. A few other eclipse chasers had begun to gather and wait, and friendly words were exchanged, but there was never a sense of crowding. People mostly stood in quiet expectation, looking east, spread out in a vaguely circular way, a human Stonehenge. There was something very ancient about it, and surreal. The air was warm, bright, and fragrant with sweet pine and dry grass. It was a golden kind of place, a golden passage into a primeval dream. We put on our cardboard-framed eclipse glasses and watched as the astronomical spectacle began.

How strange and astonishing it was to see an expanding bite taken from the orange sun, looking like a picture book illustration of a solar eclipse! I found it unexpectedly moving, inexplicably poignant. The blackness widened slowly until the narrowest crescent of light remained, and then... totality. Glasses off. I was staring directly at the sun, and the sun was blackness, both a presence and an absence, encircled by a gleaming corona. There was something shocking about it. It was like a hole in the heavens, an opening to infinity.

But the sky around it asserted itself with new vividness, and bright Venus appeared, shining like a torch. I scanned the firmament, and it was never wholly dark, and never daylight, never even dusk, but somehow blue with undertones of mauve or violet, and at the edges of the hillside there was a band of muted pink-gold light, reminiscent of dawn, but not-dawn, of here, but somewhere else. The temperature abruptly dropped, and the air was tangibly and deliciously cool, moving gently across the field like a blessing.

We were suspended in a state of enchantment. Two minutes is longer than I thought, and so I wandered, and I gazed upon the ground, where the grass had turned silvery, oddly bleached of its color, and the pine trees were ghostly, and my own familiar shadow seemed elongated and sharply etched and weirdly disconnected from my body. But maybe that's because *I* was weirdly disconnected from my body, and if this begins to sound like a hallucinogenic experience, that's probably a good way of thinking about it, because it truly was mind-altering. Even as the moon passed, and the sun reclaimed its dominion, and light and color returned to what we know, nothing seemed ordinary.

And nothing ever is. People ask me what I learned, what I felt, and it has to do with how stunningly extraordinary it is to be present to bear witness, to be alive even briefly in the fathomless universe, adrift on this beautiful and terrible planet where everything – even the commonplace – is implausible.

My first reaction as the shadow passed was pure awe, quickly followed by a profound sense of humility and gratitude, and those feelings have lingered. I am a pilgrim passing through, although I am not sure what I seek, and I have no illusions about my own significance, only an old impulse to leave things a little better, if possible, or at least try not to add to the world's collective misery. I'm still inclined to write and document too, to think out loud in search of sense, ephemeral though it is. But the universe is dancing whether we see it or not, and we can look up in wonder or miss it entirely.

I am now a woman who has seen a total eclipse, and that's something to have done in a lifetime.

As we drove home, we finally encountered the traffic that had been predicted. We came to a dead stop on a dusty road alongside a forest, the air still ashy from recent fire, and temperatures miserably hot. But people were cheerful. We had all converged in this moment in time, a moment that would never occur again, an alignment for an alignment. A driver with cables did a U-turn in the middle of the road to give a stalled car a jump start, a woman from Australia walked alongside the traffic beneath an open umbrella, a little girl was jogging with her puppy on a leash. A gentleman in a neighboring vehicle offered us a joint, and most memorably, a man with a butterfly net cavorted in the woods at the edge of the road. I don't know what he was hoping to catch, but he seemed to be having fun.

33

DAY TRIP

Our calendar was unexpectedly blank for the day. No one was counting on us, no tasks were urgent, and our irrelevance felt like license for a field trip. We recruited our old friends Kit and Beverly and set out into the misty morning.

It's a three-hour drive from here to the Carrizo Plain, a trip we traditionally make in winter, lured by the austerity and tranquility of the place. We like to wander in the silvery light and contemplate the sandstone rock formation with its mysterious Native American symbols. But it had been such an extravagant springtime! Why not glimpse Carrizo in bloom, even as it fades?

The region is located in southeastern San Luis Obispo County, and it's vast, about fifty miles long and fifteen across, the largest remaining swath of native grassland in the state. The Temblor Range borders to the northeast, and the San Andreas Fault cuts through at the foot of the mountains, exposing that most infamous break in California's topography. The alkaline Soda Lake, a central depression in the midst of the plain, receives all of the area's runoff. We accessed the plain via Soda Lake Road and walked up to a viewing point to get oriented.

Yellow-orange ribbons of bloom skirted the lake's milky shores, and a zig-zag of mountains rose in the background.

It was the kind of day that covers your skin with kisses, not the wet, sloppy kind, but light enticing kisses. Pale sun shone through sheets of fog, promising rainbows that never materialized, but we were happy with what was. Kit drove on a narrow dirt road into the hills. It was rutted and bumpy, winding around inconclusively, and we were surprised to come head-to-head with another car, driven by a woman who looked to be our age, traveling solo. Kit has been driving backcountry roads for decades and knows the protocol. He gracefully backed up until there was a little extra space, then pulled over to let the lady pass. She was grateful. "You'll see up ahead the ditch I almost went into," she said. "And I still didn't find where God spilled the paint. Have you seen it?"

We'd seen a lot already: goldfields, desert candles, owl's clover, blazing stars, tidy tips, poppies, lupines, filigree, fiddlenecks, delphinium, daisies, snake's head, and so many flowers we didn't know the names for, bright natives in full glory holding their own against invasives. Yellow prevailed, which we've observed at home as well, but as Beverly suggested, we just had to *embrace* the yellow. It was its own vibrant show, brilliantly nuanced, and quite satisfactory. But we weren't sure what the lady was referring to. "God-Spilled-the-Paint!" she shouted. "It's somewhere around here. I'm gonna find it." And off she went in a little wake of dust.

We meandered, deliciously devoid of goals. Beverly demonstrated her roadrunner mating call, a talent I never knew she had. We stopped for lunch at a campground and saw an owl in a tree. The clouds were theatrical, plush and mighty, wielding great shadows that moved by swiftly. We walked up a hill along Quail Springs Road and found thickets of fragrant gray-blue salvia and bush lupine in a washed-out shade of purple, and tiny pale blue flowers, as translucent and delicate as porcelain, and always there were those yellow expanses in the distance, surrounding us like light. A patchwork of the Central Valley was visible to the east below.

There were man-made remnants, too, all along the way: abandoned old homesteads in the far distance, eroded tanks fallen on their sides, broken fences inexplicably placed, bullet casings on the ground. Mysterious transmission towers stood on the hills like sentries, resembling stars crossed with crosses and set on stilts, almost religious.

Almost religious... as am I... or spiritual anyway, because I believe that all this glory is telling me something, even if it's just to jolt me awake. And I know this was a pilgrimage of sorts. So much beauty, so much life. With our heartbreak in one hand, and our joy in another, we fall again and again into love.

34

ROAD TRIP

Diane and I are driving east along Route 58 on our way to Las Vegas, but we'll spend our first night in a place called Newberry Springs, where we've booked lodging in a caboose. The day is sometimes rainy but mostly gray and pending, and it feels like we are driving through a cloud, with bare trees etched against the sky, and green hills giving way to brown mountains. We are comfortably ensconced in our cozy little carapace, and the miles go by.

We talk about our childhoods and our families, not happy stories, but we laugh a lot, and we know that laughter, like tears, comes with vulnerability, a gift of being open. Now James Taylor is singing "Fire and Rain", and although we're several years apart in age, we are both remembering our younger days in cold and dreary places. My husband once remarked that James Taylor and Leonard Cohen were the songwriters depressed college girls listened to in their dorms, and Diane says, "Exactly." And what would he have known of those bleak northeastern winters? He was surfing in California then, but Diane and I grew up in New York, and although it took some doing, we always knew we'd leave.

We talk about that urge to leave, the belief in its necessity, and about finding an elsewhere that becomes a home but always carrying a residue of alien-ness too, and a permanent nostalgia for things that never were. But we're good now, and consciously grateful, both of us retired from teaching and eager to learn new things. Diane is taking a woodworking class, and I wish I were brave enough to try painting, but I know I'd be terrible, and it feels too late to start at almost seventy. "Seventy gives you permission to suck," says Diane, and maybe she's right. Anything is possible. The story is ours to write.

And we talk about what teaching taught us. For me, it's still a jumble. I am grateful to know some former students in their current, grown-up lives, and I hope that I was a worthy influence, but even after all this time, I haven't quite figured out what it all meant. Diane has more clarity; she believes that the most important lesson is to try to respond, not react. "Losing my temper doesn't work," she says. "You have to keep the conversation open. You have to try to understand the source."

Understand the source – it's a useful concept. And it occurs to me that this is part of what our road trip is about. We're going to attend the Women's March rally that will be held in Las Vegas on Sunday, an event intentionally based in a "purple" state that is racially, ethnically, and politically diverse, in some ways a microcosm of Western America. The theme of the rally is "power to the polls", and it marks the launch of a monumental campaign to get the vote out.

But we're also paying homage to the mountains and the sky, to the desert and its waters, to the foundation and the source of life. In a time when so many environmental protections are under assault, we are driving back roads through country that is quietly trying to be, through landscapes that many have viewed as nothing more than potential mines and quarries and industrial sites. We are hoping to talk to a few people along the way too, maybe people who are a little different than the ones we meet at home. We'll see.

We stop by a railroad track for lunch and watch the freight trains going by. Long strands of cars, forever going by, a ubiquitous backdrop to our travels.

Judi of the Desert

We arrive before dark at Newberry Springs, a small community in the western Mojave Desert, and we find our way to Sarkasian Ranch on Route 66, where we've booked a caboose... words I never thought I'd say. The ranch is a sprawling property at the base of the mountains, dotted here and there with old railroad cars, trailers, and a handful of houses. The proprietor, Judi, comes out on a golf cart to greet us. She has a great mass of curly platinum blonde hair and a megawatt smile, and she is made up like a movie star. ("I put on my make-up every morning," she later tells us, "whether or not anyone is going to see me.")

She invites us to hop on board the golf cart and she takes us for a little tour of the premises before depositing us at our caboose. There's a fishing lake and a koi pond, a tortoise preserve and a labyrinth. There are peacocks ambling by, a baffled looking emu, and a raven named Ralphie who seems to have the run of the place. There are quirky sculptures and found treasures everywhere, and all the trees have some sort of adornment – glittery stars and owls, toy dinosaurs, and colorful plastic water pistols dangle from the branches. There's no rhyme or reason to it, just pure delight.

Judi is the undisputed queen of the domain. She describes herself as a psychologist, author, and storyteller. (Later I look her up online and discover that she is also a producer, children's entertainer, animal rescue worker, and designer of something called an "exer-chair".) She's had three husbands, is a grandmother and a great-grandmother, and believes that if you want to do something, you just have to dive in and do it. She shows us her bookstore, complete with a metaphysical room and an antique sofa from an opium den, and she talks about her plans for art activities, parties, events, and retreats.

Judi has created her own world here, and it's wacky and tacky but also brave and magnificent. She stands there in full make-up as the sun descends and the distant mountains darken, reminding me a little of the good witch Glenda. She smiles her movie star smile, and maybe there's a flicker of sadness in her eyes, but she's upright and undaunted. Her advice: "Nurture that part of yourself that is important to you, dream your dreams and be your own fairy godmother."

Diane and I sleep soundly in our red caboose, lulled by the mournful sound of distant freight trains passing in the night.

On the Road Again

In the morning, we drive just a little further along Route 66 and stop for breakfast at the Bagdad Café because it's there, and who wouldn't? It's a vintage truck stop diner made famous by the 1987 movie of the same name, which, according to Roger Ebert's review at the time of its release "walks its own strange and lovely path". Outside of the café there's a classic old motel sign, a lonely abandoned trailer, and an endless stretch of forlorn desert bleaching in the harsh glare of the sun, but within, the place is busy, cluttered with memorabilia, and noisy with talk and the clatter of plates. We walk beneath a framed picture of John Wayne to enter the restroom, then indulge in a greasy American breakfast of scrambled eggs and bacon, served by a gregarious fellow named George, who tells us that he came here decades earlier after losing his job at the Hector Mining Company.

We chat with a friendly blonde woman who is on her way to a

conference in Santa Fe; it turns out she's from Santa Barbara – we even have mutual friends. She's sorry she won't be at the rally, but she wants to get involved for the long term, and before you know it, we're standing in the Bagdad Café exchanging contact information. Meeting someone from home is not what we expected in this unlikely context, but we're allies, and life is nothing if not implausible.

There are also a couple of bikers in here, some local kids having a birthday party in a side room, a German tourist taking serious photos with a big-lens camera, and one woman in particular whose face is a deeply etched road map of hard times. She looks like someone who's had too much of some things and not enough of others, and she's feeling kind of pissed about it all. Fed and caffeinated, we hit the road.

We're about three hours from Vegas, and the highway stretches before us like a shimmering mirage. There are volcanic fields and white sand dunes, and various structures that we take to be refineries, mines, or processing plants, and above it all a breathtaking skyscape of utterly cinematic clouds. We pull over at a place called Camp Cady Wildlife Area, 1900 acres of desert riparian habitat, and we read a sign about the River Bluff Ranch on the north bank of the Mojave River. The river, which has been described as upside-down and backwards because its water generally flows below ground and inland from Silverwood Lake to Soda Dry Lake, was used by ancient indigenous people as a trade route to and from the Pacific Coast. In 1826, Jedediah Smith passed through here to become the first American to reach the California coast via an overland trail, and eventually the Mojave Road became a primary route from Los Angeles to the Arizona territory and points east.

Right now, though, there is no one in sight as far as the eye can see, and we run around under the crazy sky in the center of a two-lane highway because we can – but we begin to understand that what seems like the middle of nowhere is in fact a place of great geological and historical significance. We will encounter this kind of truth again and again as we travel. Zoom in anywhere to find a universe. There are microcosms and ecosystems within seemingly irrelevant places, there are layers of history and stories in vast swaths of silence, there are remnants of lives lived, and there is nature in all its wondrous incarnations trying to survive.

We are pilgrims. We are wonderstruck. We get back in the car for the drive to Las Vegas.

Strangers in Vegas

Las Vegas appears gradually. Heralded by billboards and buildings and increasing traffic, it spreads across the desert in all its garish dissonance. Has there ever been a city more completely removed from the natural world? We use our phone to navigate to the Golden Nugget on Fremont Street, in the heart of the old downtown. It's hard to miss. There's an extravagant arched entryway, studded with chunky gold lights, and several towers and parking structures, instantly alienating. We're staying here for convenience, and it has what we need, but we keep our heads down as we wend our way through the crowds and past maze after maze of slot machines and card tables. People seem remarkably eager to throw their money away, despite the odds, and everyone is seeking fun in a desperate sort of frenzy, but nobody looks happy.

After we check in, we go outside to take a walk, and it's interesting to see the colorful old neon signs, but there's a sordid undercurrent to it all. The area is jam-packed with drunken revelers and street performers of varying degrees of talent, among them a young man adeptly drumming on plastic buckets, a couple of acrobatic dancers, and a shaggy looking fellow holding up a sign that says, simply, "Fuck You". It saddens me to see a pale, thin, almost-naked girl standing in the chilly air of dusk advertising lap dances; she has a blank expression and looks to be younger than my daughter.

There's loud music playing, and a lot of ambitious drinking going on, and I feel as if I've stepped into the midst of a frat house party gone awry, and when someone exhales a cloud of cloyingly sweet cigar smoke directly into my face, I know I've had enough. I realize that for some this is a vacation destination, and I understand that the tourist, restaurant, and hospitality industries represent livelihoods for hundreds of thousands of people (and I must say most of the employees we interacted with were good-natured and patient), but I'm completely out of my element. We'll go to the rally tomorrow and get out of here.

The Rally

We arrive at Sam Boyd Stadium early in the day and take seats high in the bleachers. There's a festive air as women and men, young and old, drift in, many carrying colorful signs: *Voting Is My Superpower. Karma Is a Bitch, and She Votes. I Am No Longer Accepting the Things I Cannot Change; I Am Changing the Things I Cannot Accept. White Is Just My Outside Color. Respect Existence or Expect Resistance. Grab 'em by the Ballot Until They Turn Blue.* The first speaker is a Native American woman who reminds us that Las Vegas sits on native land, and that Indigenous women face a disproportionately high rate of murder and many go missing, never to be found. There are tribal dancers on the stage – to dance is to pray. Later, State Representative Paulette Jordan of Idaho, an Indigenous woman running for governor of that state, urges other women – and immigrants, and LGBT people, and

153

people with disabilities, and people of color – to run for office. First we marched, and now we run. The real Women's March will be to the polls on Election Day.

"Last year we dared to hope for a better, brighter, more inclusive world," Planned Parenthood President Cecile Richards tells us in her remarks. "This year, we're gonna go out and build it."

Voter registration and engagement is the strategy, and, as Linda Sarsour proclaims, "We will win. This is not an opinion, but a fact. We're gonna win. But I don't like to win small. We're gonna win big! The women of the U.S.A. are gonna take back America."

A young immigrant woman talks about how the government is toying with lives. A survivor of the deadly Las Vegas mass shooting speaks to us in a tremulous voice: "It's hard being here and speaking in front of a large crowd, and also scary. But doing nothing is not an option. We have a responsibility as women to register and vote on behalf of candidates who promote the issues we care about."

There are musical performances, and deeply moving songs and spoken word by Jess Flo. We see sex workers holding up red umbrellas, restaurant workers, teachers, locals, and people like us who have come from far away. There are earnest young volunteers with clipboards registering voters. "We are on assignment," Nina Turner declares. "We are called upon right now to be the change."

For me, the most rousing speaker of the day is the Reverend William Barber, his powerful voice ringing through the stadium, in the African-American oratory tradition:

"…It's time to get up and know that love can win, and justice can win, and righteousness can win when we organize black and white and brown and red and yellow; old and young; Jewish and Muslim and Christian and those who do not have a faith, but they believe in a moral agenda. It's time to get up – gay and straight. No more fighting each other. Let's fight racism. Let's fight sexism. Let's fight the extremists. It's time to get up and demand justice for all…"

He finishes in an uplifting, "Oh child, things are gonna get brighter … Because we are going to get up, get up, get up!" And we are up on our feet, cheering, shouting, singing along, hearts stirring, ready to go.

One of the speakers had earlier offered this quote from Maya Angelou: "Sometimes it's necessary to encounter defeat just so we know who we are." Well, we know who we are now. And we've all been traumatized, but as Reverend Barber said, it's time to get up. Amidst all that terrifies us and breaks our hearts, there are many things to inspire and encourage. I refuse to despair.

A Quieter Place

We leave Las Vegas the next morning. Our destination is the Amargosa River Valley at the edge of Death Valley, about eighty miles to the west but a world away, and we soon arrive at Shoshone Village on California State Route 178. A decaying old automobile is parked alongside two obsolete gasoline pumps, and there is rusting antique farm equipment scattered about on the ground, each piece with a label, an in-the-field museum of agricultural machinery. We have lunch in a little café called The Crowbar.

Afterwards, we enter the visitor center. I'm very fond of little local museums, and this one is a truly fine little haven, lovingly curated. We talk to a woman named Carla at the front desk, and she offers a wealth of knowledge about the history of the area as well as tourist information, and then we walk on wooden floors and peer into glass display cases filled with mining and railway relics, Native American artifacts, and geological displays. There are wildlife exhibits too: a coyote preserved in mid-howl, a handsome pair of ram horns, and most remarkably, there's an excavated prehistoric mammoth fossil on display in the back, like a grand finale, or an astonishing clue to mysterious beginnings that go back further than imagined. Photos and documents tell the stories of the human characters who came to seek their fortunes and build a community here, among them Ralph Jacobus Fairbanks, who founded Shoshone in 1910 as a trading post, and Charles Brown, whose granddaughter, Susan Sorrells, inherited and still owns the town.

A stone's throw from the museum is a wooden house painted green but faded into varying shades by the sun, and partially hidden by a large tamarisk tree. (We later learn that these trees, although pretty, are problematically thirsty and invasive.) Peering within, we see that the house is open to visitors, and we enter to discover the office of the Amargosa Conservancy. We browse in its sunlit front room, reading about the wild and scenic river, the many species of wildlife, and ongoing efforts to fund restoration and encourage ecotourism. We're eager to wander outdoors.

As we set out on our way, uncertain where to go, we see a young woman in a wool coat and a red bandana tied around her head, Rosie the Riveter style. We ask if she can suggest a good walking route, and indeed she can. It turns out she's the head of the Conservancy, and a delightful person too. Her name is Tanya, and she's "from the West" mostly, although she lived for a time in Iowa. Tanya gets us oriented and even walks with us to our turn-off. She's dedicated to her work and has an enthusiastic and intelligent demeanor that reminds me of one of my former students, Elise, and she is instantly relatable. I guess Tanya recognizes something familiar in Diane and me too, and she suggests an organization called Great Old Broads for Wilderness that we might consider joining. We thank her for tending to the environment, and she thanks us for going to the women's rally. (She's another ally, and she wishes she could have been there.) We like her so much that we hug her when we say good-bye, and take pictures, and say we'll be in touch.

We walk past the cemetery first, a few humble graves marked only by rotting wooden crosses, others more substantial, and many decorated with bright plastic flowers. Soon we come to the old miners' caves at Dublin Gulch, vacant but still remarkably intact, with smokestacks and wooden front doors and even bed-springs inside. From a distance, there's an eerie kind of beauty in the broken glass glittering in the sunlight, and the old rusted cans strewn upon the ground, but it's a desolate place. Carla had told us the story of a British prospector who had high tea daily in his cave, and a German bootlegger who hauled in a Victrola so he could listen to Wagner, but it's hard to imagine now. We follow a series of white poles and the contours of the rocky hills and a brushy wash, keeping sight of the oasis in the distance, and we gradually make our way back to the town.

We stop and chat with a young man named Eddie from the Nevada Conservation Corps who's working on a restoration project by a creek. The crew is focusing on a pupfish refuge, but also improving the overall habitat to enable wetlands to return. "Come back in five years and see what we've done," Eddie tells us. I hope we will. (There are good people out there, quietly doing good things.)

The Amargosa Opera House

I cannot believe I had never heard the story of Marta Becket and her opera house. A young dancer from New York, Marta was vacation camping in Death Valley with her husband in 1967, when they discovered their trailer had a flat tire. While her husband tended to repairs, Marta began to wander, drawn to a group of old adobe buildings nearby that had been constructed in the 1920s by the Pacific Coast Borax Company as part of a complex for a company town. The largest of the buildings was an abandoned theater, then called Corkhill Hall. "I can dance here," Marta thought.

"Peering through the tiny hole, I had the distinct feeling that I was looking at the other half of myself," she later wrote. "The building seemed to be saying, *Take me... do something with me... I offer you life.*"

Marta and her husband agreed to rent the theater for forty-five dollars a month, and began its transformation. Her first performance was on February 10, 1968, when she danced for an audience of twelve. But although she performed regularly three nights a week, sometimes no one came at all. Her solution: paint an audience.

It's a place of magic. Diane and I walk through the theater led by a young man named Jason who shows visitors around and works in the restaurant; he's originally from Indianapolis and lived in Los Angeles for a while, but he found his way here and it felt right to him. We are dazzled by the murals, which took four years to complete. There are kings and queens and knights, acrobats, dancers, and troubadours, angels and birds on the ceiling – a whimsical and sumptuous rendering of one woman's beautiful, madcap vision. There's something extravagantly defiant about it. Long after her husband was no longer on the scene, Marta continued to dance and paint, living on until her nineties. Her final show was February 12, 2012.

We visit the hotel, also, where Marta's artistic touch is evident in every room: trompe l'oeil paintings, decorative parrots and clowns and peacock wings on the walls, dancers and angels galore. We meet Holly, who was Marta's caregiver at the end of her life, but Holly tells us that it was Marta who cared for *her*. Standing beneath a mural of three cherubic angels, Holly shares a little about the rough times she has endured, most painfully the loss of two children; she was on the verge of giving up, but Marta had faith in her. "I think she's still looking out for me," says Holly.

I think she's still looking out for all of us, in a way. Her message is to be unafraid. Dream. Dance. Do. (Even if no one is watching.)

Tecopa and Beyond

And we go to Tecopa, of course. It's a high-energy vortex; you can sense it right away. Maybe it's the therapeutic, geothermal heated, mineral-rich hot springs, or the way the chalky salty minerals make the ground look snow-dusted, or how the mountains glow orange at dusk and the night sky blazes with stars. But maybe it's the flourishes of quirky creative humans: a purple-painted kiosk, an old truck rusted and peeling into multiple hues and abandoned in a field like an art installation, or in one place the twinkle of tiny red and green lights in the trees and the air, so it's like walking through a fairyland, and it isn't even Christmas. We take a dip in the silky waters of the hot spring pool at Delight's bathhouse and enjoy a fabulous meal at Eric Scott's Steaks and Beer, a gourmet restaurant in the proverbial middle of nowhere.

But speaking of meals, I would be remiss if I didn't mention El Valle Restaurant in Amargosa Valley, where we stopped for Mexican food, including homemade tortillas, and it was top-notch. El Valle is run by a lovely lady named Ampara, whose Christmas tree is still standing in the entryway, but it's been redecorated as a New Year's tree, because 2018 is going to be a great year, and in a couple of weeks she plans to turn it into a Valentine's Day tree, because, as Ampara is fond of saying, "Why not?"

Is there a theme to our wanderings? Today I think it would be about daring to aspire and create and having the freedom to do so.

There'd be something about resilience, too – and the spirit of why not.

The Ash River Wilderness Preserve

Our trip culminates at the Ash River Wilderness Preserve, and it's the perfect place to be still and contemplate, the perfect place from which to return. We take the boardwalk path and look upon a crystal clear aquamarine stream. From the bottom, nearly fifteen feet down, 2,800 gallons of fresh water is flowing to the surface and collecting in limestone bedrock. This aquifer has given life to fish, animals, and humans for eons. Ancient Indigenous tribes saw this as the holy and sacred place it is, and they came from miles away and all directions to gather here.

In 1980, a corporation proposed turning this place into a development that would include hotels, strip malls, an airport, and over 30,000 homes. Why drive to Las Vegas, when you can bring Las Vegas here? Thankfully, vigilant citizens stood up and fought it, and today Ash Meadows is a wildlife refuge.

We stood at the source. And today, as always, there was the water, and the wild heart of the desert, trying to be.

35

BROKEN OPEN

I mounted my trusty bicycle just like old times. I had pedaled only a few feet up the road when I heard a vehicle approaching from behind me, but as I turned my head slightly to look back and assess, my bike tipped over and I toppled to the ground, bruising limbs and self-esteem. It was a necessary wake-up call. The gods hate hubris, after all, and I had not believed or understood until this moment the very real physical repercussions of my impairments. After brain surgery, I live my life in a state of disequilibrium, recalibrating constantly. I am completely deaf in one ear, neurologically stressed, easily fatigued, and minus a balance nerve.

But the hardest part in the initial months following the operation was mental: debilitating insomnia, anxiety, and depression. I had jokingly referred to the surgery beforehand as "the grand opening" – little did I know how scarily open and vulnerable I would soon feel. As the muting effects of sedation and steroids faded, a sense of shock and panic set in, and I was to struggle with these for months. I was simply unable to believe that I would ever feel better, and I faced each day with dread.

"If this is my new life," I said to Monte one morning, "I don't want it."

"You ingrate," he replied, and I don't blame him. He was trying so hard to pull me back.

It had all begun with an acoustic neuroma. "These tumors are tricky," said the doctor when it was first discovered, but it was benign and small, and its only discernible effect was diminished hearing in my left ear, and I didn't think I'd ever have to deal with it. However, three years of MRIs revealed that it was growing, and beginning to touch a band of nerve fibers that connects the cerebellum to the brainstem. A specialist in Los Angeles told me that my watch-and-wait window had expired, and that I needed to choose between radiation and surgery. "Think about it," he said, "but not for too long." It was a decision I felt unqualified to make, but after months of research and agonizing, I opted for the surgery. I wanted the thing *out*, unequivocally.

The type of operation I had is called a translabyrinthine craniotomy, a delicate micro-surgery in which the semicircular canals and vestibule of the inner ear are removed with a surgical drill to get to the tumor, which was located on a cranial nerve, at which point a neurosurgeon steps in to perform the actual task of cutting it away. Fat extracted from my stomach was used to plug up the hole inside my head, and the flap around my ear, having been opened like a doorway, was stitched neatly shut. It took about nine hours, after which I was wheeled into the ICU, where I spent a few days in a state of suspended animation. I have seen my scar only in a photograph taken days afterwards, ruby-beaded horseshoe-shaped stitchery extending from behind my ear on the left side of my head. It was impressive.

After about a week, I was allowed to go home. I reclined in the passenger seat, my head nestled in pillows, as we inched our way north through the traffic of Los Angeles and the San Fernando Valley, then into Santa Barbara, and eventually the rural outpost of Gaviota. At last I was in my own dear room, in my own dear bed, looking out at the familiar hills.

And I thought the worst was over, but I was mistaken – the craziness was about to begin. As I became aware of all the changes and sensations that were now a part of my life, I grew increasingly distressed, anxiety that exploded into heart-pounding panic attacks and terrible insomnia. The psychiatrist described me as traumatized, wondered why I was reacting so viscerally, and suggested that I strive for "post-traumatic growth", but I was stalled. I felt a profound sense of loss, as if my former self had died. I had gone into the hospital feeling fine and come out broken, with the limitations of a ninety-year-old.

The California winter kept hurtling towards springtime. On beautiful days that were misty and green, I forced myself to get up and step outside. Then rain came, and the leaves in the orchard glistened, and everything was wet and drippy. It rained steadily, sometimes straight down, but sometimes sideways when the wind picked up, and I spent these days indoors. I lay adrift in my bed-raft, looking out at the changing colors of the sea and sky and Santa Rosa Island, waiting for time to pass.

I became obsessively self-aware. I had never understood how many micro-adjustments are involved in every moment of being alive. I was grateful to know the tumor was gone, but at the same time, the stitches felt tight and tingly, and everything was half again as quiet, and I was weak and tired in a way I'd never felt before. Sometimes

I felt a stuffiness inside my head, but sometimes it was more of an emptiness, an avenue with no traffic. My left eye was painfully dry, and I couldn't focus in order to read. Even my sense of taste was altered, and my appetite was gone. I was uncomfortable and unfamiliar to myself, as if a stranger had invaded and inhabited my body. My nervous system frequently bolted into a state of fight or flight, sending out galloping surges of adrenalin, and in these moments, I was terrified and crazed.

I have no illusions about how much I was suffering. Beloved members of my own family of origin endured the ravages of acute and chronic physical illness far beyond my own ability to imagine it. They were stoic and brave, fighting back as they could, but by and large consigned to the cruel randomness of their allotted fates, while I so casually inhabited my haven of perfect health, free to take it all for granted. What I was feeling would have likely been a pretty good day for my sister, for example, probably one of her best. But suffering is relative, and when it is happening to you, it feels real enough.

And while the twinges and aches in my head would not have qualified as serious pain, a sick, queasy feeling at the core of me never went away, and each day loomed ahead like a trial, not a gift. I knew of folks who seemed to traverse the recovery path with relative ease simply by resting a lot, being patient, and having faith in their body's own healing. Unfortunately, I lacked the ability to trust or to sleep, and when anxiety set in, it seemed to override everything else. Even in my calmer periods, I felt bewildered and exhausted as my brain worked to compensate for all the vestibular changes. That constant recalibration and accommodation brings on what is referred to as "neuro-fatigue", and it is real and chronic.

"What do you do for fun?" the psychiatrist asked me, for which I had no answer. I was told it would take a year to recover, but a year seemed abstract and eternal, and I did not believe that I could possibly get through it.

I had a different sense of time. Maybe I thought time was linear, but now it seemed more like a web in which we float, each of us separate, but connected as well. Internal, external, depends how you look at it. I was on a raft on a river, carried along by a current, but I didn't know where the shore was. Sometimes my goal was to simply lean back and not hurt, to somehow move from one moment to the next. How long did this go on? A few months, but it felt like forever.

One day I heard a podcast interview with poet and psychologist Anita Barrows, in which she said, "Suddenly, in depression, you are ripped from what felt like your life, from what felt right and familiar and balanced and ordinary and ordered, and you're just thrown into this place where you're ravaged, where the wind rips the leaves from the trees, and there you are – very, very much the soul in depression." I recognized myself in this description. Whether situational or physiological, I could not deny that I was seriously depressed.

I went to traditional doctors and psychologists, listened to meditation tapes, tried acupuncture and massage and homeopathic remedies, shopped Amazon for weighted blankets, vitamin supplements, preservative-free eye drops, vile tasting tea, books about sleep hygiene and anxiety phobia. I got my medical marijuana card online and entered a vaulted dispensary on a back street in town in the futile hope that a slim young man in dreadlocks would help me to find effective cannabis assistance. I tapped into my teachers' retirement fund to hand wads of cash to the psychiatrist whom I fervently hoped would lead me back to health. I declined well-meaning invitations for even low-key kinds of socializing. I was utterly miserable – tedious, obsessive, and fatalistic – and I scared people away.

I cherish those who checked in anyway. My friend Diane came by, smelling of the beautiful outdoors. She cooked us dinner and assured me that there would still be lots of activism for us take on when I was strong again. Barb wrote to me from snowy Saratoga. Jeanne reminded me about our post-rain walks in the canyon. My sister-in-law Lindy, a cancer survivor, welcomed me into the fellowship of strong women. There were so many flowers in my room, and so many kinds of sweets, baskets filled with socks and lotions, books, and bread, and jars of broth. My husband was a constant presence, and I was grateful for my own odd and complicated family of origin, who were here for me in their own ways, checking in from faraway with concern and advice and affection.

Kindnesses and messages arose from unexpected sources. Once, while in my darkest depths, I was hiding in the downstairs room while everyone else seemed to be out and about enjoying life. The phone rang, and it was my young friend Nyuol, calling me from New York, and he described vignettes of Harlem to me that he could see that very moment through the window of his brownstone apartment. He took me away for a few minutes. Another time, Kit and Beverly invited us over to their house, and it was perfectly okay with them that I lay on the couch and didn't say much, looking at Kit's beautiful little pastel landscapes and skyscapes pinned to the wall. Hilary-of-Wales thought of me and sent me a letter in the early hours of morning. Jan, who was going through a trial of her own, checked in daily and we talked about how we would rejoin the resistance when this was over, and maybe get our nails done too. A woman named Bonny whom I barely know and had met at the *On Being* gathering earlier this year sent me David Whyte's newest poetry book. And my poet-friend Dan sent me an email asking me to read the lines Wordsworth composed about Tintern Abbey. I zoomed in on these words, daring to hope:

While here I stand, not only with the sense
Of present pleasure, but with pleasing thoughts
That in this moment there is life and food
For future years. And so I dare to hope,
Though changed, no doubt, from what I was, when first
I came among these hills…

And the moon kept beaming down on the hills, serene and oblivious, and one day I pedaled a short distance on my bike and didn't fall over, and I was changed, but I began to suspect that summer would come, and all seasons in their turn, and somehow I would be looking back at this as a hard but necessary time.

I will always remember that the springtime was extravagantly beautiful, the hillsides outrageously yellow, everything in raucous bloom, and I was removed from it all. I missed the cycles of the moon, the push and pull of tides, the blazing of stars, the shifts of light and changes in the sky as days lengthened.

Bright yellow orioles began appearing at the honeysuckle, spreading their wings in sumptuous flashes of color. I walked defiantly up the canyon in howling wind, then leaned against an oak tree. "I am still here," I told myself.

I began to recall details from when I was in the hospital. One day, at the nadir of my misery, I had looked up and seen Monte standing there, and a sense of love and humility and gratitude had filled me to the core of my being. But of course, being Cynthia-the-haunted, I had suddenly flashed back to an image of my poor mother, lying in her narrow bed not long before she died, and the appreciation and love that registered on her face when she looked up to see me, and that memory made me start to cry, because I knew I meant that much to her, and I wasn't there enough. And then I remembered that we are never there enough, and we can never do enough, but that is not the point. I felt love as a force, not a means but the thing itself, and I saw it as real and powerful and everlasting. It is the animus, the spirit, the eternal, the energy of what we may even choose to call God.

Here I am, sounding religious again, but I have been stripped of my usual coping mechanisms and I can no longer busy myself with this and that, pivoting from the sadness, avoiding confrontation with the mystery. What becomes of all the words and thoughts? What deeds will have mattered? I am telling you what was left, and what was real to me. And why do I feel compelled to write about this? My answers are questions: How much can we contain in silence? And why should we keep it to ourselves? Do we not matter to one another? Do we not hunger for connection?

If anyone is listening, thank you.

But there was so much learning to be done. Dian, a Ranch neighbor who was in a terrible car accident more than a decade ago, reached out to me and offered to be a mentor. Having endured more than her share of suffering with extraordinary spirit, her insights were hard-won and valuable. She wrote:

"You will learn to move forward and find the best path to begin this momentous journey of healing not only your body but your spirit, and the taking back of your life. Will it be the same as before? Probably not, but that is what life is: an ever-changing landscape. Sometimes we gracefully traverse it and at other moments we are miserably crawling around, looking outward for a reprieve, for we are drawn to that easy beautiful path, but my toughest moments are the ones that brought me the most insight. I have crossed a desert of pain and hopelessness, not always gracefully, but like that ugly duckling my time has come at last... I am a swan! Yes, there are tough days, but there are many more good ones, and I live those fully. There are some things I can no longer do, although I have done my best to try, but I have stretched my wings and found new avenues to travel which I never would have known existed without having had my chain yanked! My dearest, you have had your chain yanked. Now thank the universe that you have been given a chance to live more fully and with more gusto, taking chances you never thought you might, because you now will grow an inward strength you did not know you owned."

Yes, I have had my chain yanked. But it is from Dian that I began to understand that life is also how we look at it, how we respond to the twists and turns and challenges, even the scary ones, that I could label pain as "sensation", plough through discomfort and accept it simply as the way it feels to be alive, and reinvent myself – from a broken being to someone new, wise, compassionate, and grateful. Dian was living evidence. I started to believe that I *would* heal, that it would take some time, but I could adapt and adjust and grow.

One afternoon I was upstairs in my little room, lying on a yoga mat with the intent of stretching and meditating, but really just lying on a yoga mat. Suddenly I had the feeling that I was not alone, and there on the deck was a bobcat, a particularly large and beautiful one. He looked at me while I looked at him, then he casually ambled off. When I told this story to Dan, he said, "The bobcat allowed you to see him because you were worthy and awake. It sounds like you are seeing again. I mean really seeing."

Maybe it's true. And with this kind of seeing, boundaries dissolve. A page of Dan's book *Particles* falls open, and I read: "Is a honey bee one being, or an element of one being?" It's a matter of perspective. I am becoming someone who sees omens, symbols, totems. I embrace the irrational. I think of the ancient arrowhead dislodged by my heel as I walked up the canyon a month before my surgery, the prayer flags placed for me by friends of friends somewhere in the foothills of the Himalayas, the wren song in the morning, this very room filled with light, and a bobcat gazing into it. Why should I not accept all these as significant and personal? I have spent too much time bound by barriers and constructs.

I had reached a turning point. It's an especially fitting term because so much of this experience has been about turning and learning to move, in particular turning my head deliberately, repeatedly, and rapidly to facilitate my vestibular readjustment, and turning my body to loosen up and possibly revive the memories of joyful motion. Some of the exercises felt absurd, but I had been reassured that they help, and I was putting my faith in all sorts of things. I had succumbed to Big Pharma, too, adding a low dose of an SSRI antidepressant to my daily routine, something I had managed to avoid all my life, but even if this didn't significantly turn me around, it certainly didn't hurt. And I walked outdoors in backcountry and beach, pushing myself further each day, even if I felt like I had just stepped off a merry-go-round. *If drinking is bitter, change yourself to wine...* that's what Rilke said. And I was determined to do just that. I would postpone both fun and duty, and this would be the year I dedicated to saving my life.

I knew I had a long road ahead, but my spirit and determination were returning. I still felt precarious at times, still had difficult days, and I never did take sleep for granted, but I saw what I was dealing with, and I was figuring out how to cope, even if coping just meant getting used to it. And there were unexpected bonuses from having been to the dark place. The writer Andrew Solomon expressed this idea with eloquence when talking about his own experience with depression: "I think the awareness of my own vulnerability has made me more aware of other people's vulnerability and more appreciative of people who cushion me from the things to which I am vulnerable. So I think it's made me both more loving and more receptive to love and given me a clearer sense than I would otherwise have had of the value of love. And I suppose – again, without wanting to get into a suggestion of specific doctrine, but that has also given me a sense that some abstract love in the world, which I suppose we could call the love of God, is essential and significant."

I was seeing a theme. I too had a growing sense of love in the world, both abstract and tangible, essential, and significant.

I walk along the canyon road nearly every morning. Sometimes I walk in a mindful way, trying to notice everything around me, and sometimes I listen to podcasts or let my thoughts wander where they will. Letting thoughts wander where they will can be a dangerous prospect, but I am also learning to redirect, avoid traps, and make spaces for stillness, and these are important new skills.

There's a lot going on out there and right here. Yesterday white fog blurred hilltops, a tiny garter snake slid with speed and stealth across the path, and a canyon wren sang its beautiful song as I passed. I learned that twelve new moons had been discovered orbiting Jupiter, and that rising sea levels might affect internet infrastructure. I heard more disturbing news about the current regime and the bizarre creature who is supposedly Our president, then quickly switched over to *On Being* and savored an interview with the wonderful Luis Alberto Urrea: "A deep truth of our time is that we miss each other." I couldn't agree more fully.

Another lesson learned is that I am absolved. No more beating up on myself. I have suffered enough. I've been a good enough, well-meaning person, and I don't intend to waste any more precious life energy flagellating myself and dwelling on sadness and regret.

Also, I have learned that we get to choose what owns us: I can focus on an unpleasant feeling and let it dominate the day, or I can label it differently and pay attention to something worthier. We are all getting older, all changing. There are things I cannot do. That's not the most important thing about me.

I am learning that I will get through this. It was just a little harder than expected. And I won't be the same, but in some ways, I'll be better.

I have learned to be more understanding of the suffering of others.

I have learned about gratitude and humility.

I've learned that I have some remarkable, kind, and gracious people in my life, and I'm learning to be helped.

I'm learning that I still like the way sunlight fades the paint on an old wooden house, and how the yellow grass is turning russet, and that if I happen to look up at night, I see a sky powdery with white stars so wondrous it's hard to imagine they are not singing us all awake.

In July, I went to Los Angeles for a follow-up post-surgical exam. "Everything looks good," said the internist. "Go home and finish healing," said the surgeon. We walked around the city, and I noticed things and took pictures, and felt that I had rejoined the procession of life. There was a photography exhibit in the public library near our hotel, and a poem called "Reality Demands" by Wislawa Szymborska was mounted on the wall. It was about how, despite tragedy and misery, joy and wonder persist. I copied these lines from the poem into my journal:

On the tragic mountain passes

the wind blows hats off heads
and we cannot help –
but laugh.

I have since heard the sound of my own long-absent laughter, and occasionally I sing… badly, but I do. One afternoon as I walked solo on the beach I came upon a large, green, very bouncy beach ball snagged in the kelp, about to be pulled out to sea to become pollution. I heroically ventured into the damp water's edge and pulled it out, then kicked it along as I walked. Sometimes it bounced a bit and went far. Sometimes it started rolling back into the water and I had to run after it. This went on for quite a while. I suddenly had a purpose. What's more, it dawned on me that I was having fun chasing the green ball. Actual fun! Then followed the realization that I need more frivolity and play in my life. I gave the ball to the first kid I saw, a girl who was thrilled to have it, whose mom said they'd bring it home and make sure it didn't end up in the ocean. But here's to fun. I want some more of that.

I've never been a big fan of the idea of a "bucket list", but I did have a few things that I wanted to do while still reasonably able-bodied – see the Northern Lights, that sort of thing. It's funny now how simple my desires are. I have but one item on my bucket list for travel. I want to be on my daughter's street in Oxford, stepping outside that familiar red door, with her and Monte and Xander, and it will be one of those early summer nights when the sky is still bright white at nearly ten o'clock, and we'll be walking over to the Cowley Road for take-out, and afterwards, we'll hug goodnight, and Monte and I will walk back over to Neal and Dot's flat arm in arm, and the percussion of our footsteps on the sidewalk will punctuate the night, along with snippets of conversation from passersby, and in the morning Miranda will call and we'll meet for coffee. I don't really need to go anyplace else.

I hereby proclaim: I will give things away. I will be kinder than I ever was before. I'll take nothing for granted, and I will never succumb to despair.

Remind me that I said this.

36

THE WAY IT WAS

This is a primary source document, a transcription of what it felt like to be alive in this time and place. It was an era of disillusionment, greedy and destructive men were empowered, the gap between rich and poor was widening, and our environment was in peril. Many of us woke up in a state of disbelief about what was happening to our country. We worried, and we did a lot of hand-wringing, and looked for ways to make a difference, but sometimes it all seemed overwhelming. We tried. We meant well.

At the same time, I enjoyed the day. I recognized that I was a person of privilege, buffered from immediate adversity, a person who had the luxury of taking long walks and reading books, someone who could wake up in the morning and ask myself what I felt like doing.

And often what I did was of no consequence.

Trains passed through, like caravans of light, and if I were near the tracks, I waved. I baked bread and wrote pages that no one will read. Mars reached opposition to the sun and was closer and brighter than it had been in many years, a steady red-hued lantern above the hills. I lay on the ground alongside my daughter one night looking up at the Milky Way, and we saw a shooting star. My peers began to turn seventy. Children I once taught grew up and traveled the world, and some had children of their own. An old friendship ended, a casualty of the great political divide, and new friendships took me by surprise. Kappy and I stood outside Jacopo's door one afternoon and heard him playing the piano. Anne knitted socks, and Andy rode the waves. A few people still wrote letters and mailed them in envelopes with stamps, but these were increasingly rare.

There were protests and concerts. Hurricanes hit. A small town raised money to open a public library. My high school class held a fiftieth anniversary reunion on Long Island, but I didn't go. The citrus trees yielded fruit in abundance, and I had fresh-squeezed orange juice daily. Social media technology was monetized and weaponized, and all of us were vulnerable. An archbishop was canonized. A journalist was murdered.

Sometimes I remembered the cold north, not just the misery of it, but black ice and diamond nights, and the way it was when snow first fell and everything felt new and forgiven. Sometimes I thought about how spring would dribble in, with its smells of rain and puddled mud, the lacy chartreuse buds of trees, lilacs in bloom. And I remembered a time when everyone I loved was still alive. But sometimes I stepped straight into the moment in front of me, and didn't look back, and it was more than sufficient.

My farmer friend planted squash and tomatoes, and a retired teacher I know tutored children after school. Diane did her best to help get out the vote. Poems were written. Plastic bags were banned. Ernie Pico taught dance to senior citizens. People gathered for poetry readings and community meetings. School kids came to see the tidepools, one man built grandfather clocks from the wood of downed oak trees, and a cowgirl bottle-fed an orphaned calf. In some circles, kindness and civility still mattered. Money was raised for good causes.

I've been gathering acorns. I want to try growing an oak. If even one takes root, I'll be thrilled. Last year my neighbor gathered 200, went through all the motions, and ended up with zero seedlings. But I like knowing the potential exists.

I had a Facetime chat with my daughter in Oxford the other day, mildly distracted by a hummingbird darting about the brush. Suddenly my daughter paused, looked out the window of her house, and smiled.

"What are you seeing?" I asked.

"A man on a unicycle," she said. "He's playing a harmonica and a ukulele as he pedals down the street."

Why not? These things happen.

ACKNOWLEDGEMENTS & PERMISSIONS

Grateful acknowledgement is made to Canterbury Press, for permission to reprint an excerpt of the essay "Oremus" by Pádraig Ó Tuama, from his book *Daily Prayer with the Corrymeela Community,* 2017.

Grateful acknowledgement to A.A. Knopf for permission to use an excerpt of the poem "Physics" by Sharon Olds, which appeared in a collection called *The Wellspring,* 1995.

Grateful acknowledgement to Graywolf Press for permission to use an excerpt from "You Reading This, Be Ready" by William Stafford, from *Ask Me: 100 Essential Poems.* Copyright © 1980, 1998 by William Stafford and the Estate of William Stafford. Reprinted with the permission of The Permissions Company, Inc. on behalf of Graywolf Press, Minneapolis, Minnesota, www.graywolfpress.org.

Song lyrics quoted: "Tuesday Afternoon" by the Moody Blues, originally released on 1967 album *Days of Future Passed*; "As Tears Go By" (written by Jagger/Richards/Oldham) and released as a single by Marianne Faithfull in 1964; "Gonna Get Through This World", words by Woody Guthrie, 1945, copyright Woody Guthrie Publications, Inc.; "Bridges and Balloons" by Joanna Newsom from *The Milk-Eyed Mender,* 2004.

Immeasurable thanks to my gracious readers and encouragers Jan Brown, Jerry DiPego, Vickie Gill, Dorothy Jardin, and Diane Seigal-Doud, and to Dan Gerber, for his mentorship and guidance over the years, and to my son-in-law, Xander Cansell, who so generously stepped up when I was feeling overwhelmed by the publishing process, and to my daughter, Miranda Ward Cansell, for her brilliant editing and so much more.

Thanks to Arlyn Nathan, for the cover design, and the gifts of her expertise and kindness. And to Kappy Wells, for the cover drawing, and for bringing adventure back into our neighborhood.

Thanks also to The Book Loft, a true old-fashioned bookshop in Solvang, California, for letting me be famous for a moment in my little community.

Thanks to Vickie and Cornelia, for crucial catharsis and camaraderie via the Bestie Line and in person.

And a special hug to Oralee Kiewit, one of my most loyal readers, who, with the wisdom and authority of the nonagenarian that she is, convinced me that my work has merit, and urged me to get busy and *write!*

All along the way, I have been helped and nurtured by friends and beloveds too numerous to list here, but they are present on every page and in my heart forever.

About The Author

Cynthia Carbone Ward is a former teacher, a Fellow of the South Coast Writing Project, co-founder of The Gaviota Writers' Group, a frequent contributor to The Santa Barbara Independent, and creator of an oral history project, *The Living Stories Collective* (www.livingstoriescollective.com), an ongoing labor of love. A native of New York, she has lived with her husband Monte on a California cattle ranch for twenty-five years, a fact that still amazes her. This is her fourth book.

CPSIA information can be obtained
at www.ICGtesting.com
Printed in the USA
LVHW042029300420
654645LV00006B/410

9 780578 434636